VENICE
CULT RECIPES

LAURA ZAVAN

VENICE
CULT RECIPES

PHOTOGRAPHY BY GRÉGOIRE KALT

MURDOCH BOOKS

PREFACE

When my friends come back from Venice and tell me about their trip, I often discover they have not tasted the 'ma-gni-fi-co' *baccalà mantecato*, the sardines *in saor*, the *seppie al nero* ... I wanted to write this book to introduce you to the culinary world of Venice, so on your next visit to *La Serenissima*, you can stroll through its markets, taste its real cuisine and the incredible variety of seasonal vegetables grown in saline soils, and discover the treasure that is the seafood of the lagoon with its legendary flavour. (*La Serenissima* was the name for the Republic of Venice, an independent state until the late eighteenth century.) This cuisine will surprise you. Its wealth and variety reflect the numerous relationships the city has developed over the centuries with the populations of cities such as Rome and Byzantium, and a variety of cultures: the Jewish traditions and those from trading posts in Istria, Dalmatia ... My recipes are drawn from tradition and from secrets shared by Venetian friends and restaurateurs, whom I name and thank at the end of the book. This book is an easy way to keep the memory of all those flavours alive once you get back home. Just make sure you use quality ingredients for maximum flavour.

THE HISTORY

Venice is a magic city, an 'inverted forest', as Tiziano Scarpa suggests in his book *Venice is a Fish*. It is built on millions of tree trunks connecting a group of small islands (imagine: over a million trunks hold up the Madonna della Salute church). Born to defend itself against invasions and for trade—firstly through the sale of salt, then spices—Venice became the key launching point for all the conquests in the Mediterranean. Venice *is* a fish: look at its shape. A fish that has travelled far, bringing back riches and knowledge to become a dominant economic power for centuries. Then came the decline. Venice went from being a trading city to a city of pleasure and gambling, where *Carnevale* lasted six months (see the memoirs of Casanova).

THE CITY

La Serenissima is unique. It reveals its true nature to we twenty-first-century land-dwellers who lose ourselves in its alleyways far from the crowds. Venice soothes us and makes us rediscover slowness and beauty. It awakens our senses and takes us on a journey. And when the wanderer gets hungry, Venice is there to invite you to its table, call you into its *bàcari* (wine bars) and restaurants, where it is recommended you give in to pleasure and indulgence. To 'go to the *bàcari*', the Venetians say '*andare a bàcàri*'. This is a social activity you develop a taste for very quickly! I suggest you practise it several times a day to steep yourself in the atmosphere of Venice. Each one has its own particular ambience, which has a lot to do with the owners and their regulars. The spectacle is all around you. The atmosphere is warm. It's where people meet—friends and strangers. Venice is a magic city for the curious-minded. It's up to each individual to choose 'their' Venice.

TABLE OF CONTENTS

ON THE CICHETI MENU

IL BÀCARO
& I CICHETI
VENETIAN–STYLE APERITIFS

The ancestor of fast food and happy hour, the Venetian *bàcaro*, whose origins date back to the mid-nineteenth century, is the working person's wine bar. It's where they go to indulge in a variety of little dishes, Venetian-style *tapas*, at any time of day. It's also the meeting place for the *aperitivo*–pre-dinner drinks. One of the meanings of 'bàcaro wine' is 'wine for celebrating' ... You drink little glasses of wine called 'shadows', or spritzes, and you sample the *cicheti*, literally 'little things', set out on the counter: sardines *in saor, folpetti, baccalà mantecato* with polenta, *polpette* ...

BACCALÀ

Il baccalà (Gadus morhua) holds the record for fish sales in the region. It is rehydrated dried cod, also called merluzzo. It is ubiquitous on the counters of the bàcari as an aperitif, but it is also served as a salad or main dish.

An important clarification: in Italy, baccalà is the name for salt cod, and dried cod is referred to as stockfish (stoccafisso or stocco in the South). But be careful, because in Veneto (the Italian region of which Venice is the capital), the term baccalà is used to refer to both dried cod and salt cod dishes, without distinguishing between them. However, almost all of the baccalà dishes you see there are based on dried cod.

Dried cod was introduced to Venetian cuisine in the first half of the fifteenth century, after captain Pietro Querini's boat and crew were shipwrecked in the Lofoten islands in the Norwegian Sea. The sailors were taken in by the fishermen of the village of Røst, where they learned the techniques for fishing, drying (two months in the open air) and preparing dried cod, which they then brought back home. The dried fish was a huge success, thanks to its long shelf life and flavour. By imposing meat-free days on Christians, the Council of Trent (1561) further enhanced its status. The first recipes using dried cod date from 1570, in the Opera of Bartolomeo Scappi, the cook for Pope Pius V, who left us a bible of over a thousand recipes, including some based on dried cod, called 'merlucce secche'. From the seventeenth century onwards, il baccalà has been one of the most loved and popular dishes in Venice.

HOW TO PREPARE IT

To cook dried cod, you first need to rehydrate it for 4–5 days in water, changing the water several times a day. In Veneto, it is sold already rehydrated (bagnata) because it is used regularly, except in the warmest months. Dried cod, which has lost 70% of its weight, is still very high in protein, vitamins, iron and calcium and, once rehydrated, doubles in weight. Allow 100 g (3½ oz) dried cod per person. Choose white-fleshed dried cod ('ragno', from the name of the Norwegian exporter), which is better quality.

In the absence of dried cod (which is difficult to find outside of Italy), I've used salt cod in the recipes in this book. The texture is different, the flavour is not as pronounced but I think the result is satisfactory.
- If you buy whole salt cod, it needs to be desalted and rehydrated for 2–3 days in water, changing the water several times a day.
- If you buy fillets of salt cod, 24 hours soaked in water should be enough (don't forget to change the water several times).
- If you buy flaked salt cod, allow 30 minutes or more, depending on the thickness of the pieces.
- Otherwise you can buy ready-to-use frozen desalted cod.

BACCALÀ MANTECATO

CREAMED DRIED COD (MY RECIPE)

This is a very delicious dried cod 'cream'. It's my favourite cicheto!

SERVES 6 DESALTING TIME: 30 MINUTES TO 12 HOURS
PREPARATION TIME: 30 MINUTES COOKING TIME: 5 MINUTES

300 g (10½ oz) desalted cod*
1 bay leaf
1 garlic clove (see garlic note below)
1 handful of flat-leaf (Italian) parsley, leaves and stalks separated
150 ml (5 fl oz) grapeseed or sunflower oil, or more if necessary
2½ tablespoons olive oil
2-3 anchovy fillets, chopped, or 1 tablespoon salted capers, rinsed

Cover the cod with cold water in a saucepan and add the bay leaf, garlic clove
and parsley stalks. Bring to the boil and simmer for 5 minutes. Skim the surface,
remove from the heat and cover. Let the fish cool in the water for 20 minutes, then
drain. Flake the flesh carefully between your fingers to remove all the bones. Put
the flaked flesh in the bowl of a food processor with a plastic blade or an electric
mixer with a paddle. Mix while slowly adding the oils in a thin stream, as for a
mayonnaise, and beat together thoroughly until you have a creamy consistency.
The amount of oil needed depends on the quality of the fish—its fat content—and
the quantity of oil the fish absorbs. Add the chopped parsley leaves, anchovy
and season if necessary. Serve on a slice of grilled polenta, or a *crostino*.

TIPS

If you prefer a lighter cream, replace some of the oil with cooking water.
If you don't have an electric mixer, use a wooden spoon and mix vigorously in one
direction while adding the oil.

NOTE

In Venice this recipe would be made with dried cod, which is sold already
rehydrated, since it is used so often. If you buy dried cod (my advice is to buy it
vacuum-packed), allow 4-5 days in water to rehydrate it, changing the water several
times a day, then cook it as for salt cod.

GARLIC NOTE

Older garlic may have green sprouts which can taste bitter and should be removed.
To do this cut the garlic clove in half and remove the sprout with a small knife.

* See page 11 for how to prepare salted cod.

CROSTINI

WITH DRIED COD THREE WAYS

*Cut a baguette-style loaf into 1 cm (½ inch) slices and toast them before topping with three sorts of baccalà. For the recipe for **baccalà mantecato**, see page 12, for **baccalà alla vicentina**, see the recipe on page 148. The recipe for **baccalà alla cappuccina** is below.*

BACCALÀ ALLA CAPUCCINA

DRIED COD SALAD

<u>SERVES 6 PREPARATION TIME:</u> 20 MINUTES <u>COOKING TIME:</u> 20 MINUTES

1 kg (2 lb 4 oz) rehydrated or desalted cod*
4 garlic cloves, halved
1 handful of flat-leaf (Italian) parsley stalks
1 small handful of flat-leaf (Italian) parsley leaves, chopped
Olive oil, to serve

Rinse the cod well. Place it in a saucepan and cover with water. Add the garlic and parsley stalks. Bring to the boil and simmer for 15 minutes. Drain the cod and let it cool in a mixing bowl. Remove the skin and bones. Flake it coarsely with a fork and toss with the oil, salt, pepper and parsley. Serve on a crostino or with a salad.

OVEN-BAKED VERSION

This variation comes from a very old recipe. Sauté the garlic and parsley in oil then combine them with the dried cod, which has been rehydrated and poached for 10 minutes beforehand. Put everything into a baking dish and cover with milk. Once it's cooked, add raisins and pine nuts.

* See page 11 for how to prepare dried or salted cod.

BACCALÀ FRITTO

FRIED DRIED COD

Have with drinks or as a main dish, like a kind of fish and chips ... But in Venice, it's just baccalà, without the chips!

SERVES 6 PREPARATION TIME: 30 MINUTES
COOKING TIME: 15 MINUTES RESTING TIME: 10 MINUTES

Mix **200 ml (7 fl oz) of soda water** with **1 egg** and **100 g (3½ oz) of plain (all-purpose) flour**. Beat everything together and let the batter rest for 10 minutes. Place **500 g (1 lb 2 oz) of desalted cod** (see page 11) in a saucepan, cover with **500 ml (17 fl oz/2 cups) of milk** and bring to the boil. Remove from the heat, drain and cut into 5 cm (2 inch) pieces. In a deep-fryer or large heavy-based saucepan, heat **1 litre (35 fl oz/4 cups) of vegetable oil** to 180°C (350°F), or until a cube of bread dropped into the oil turns golden brown in 15 seconds. Dip the pieces of cod in the batter and deep-fry them until golden. Serve with lemon wedges.

UOVO SODO & ACCIUGA

HARD-BOILED EGG & ANCHOVIES

This cicheto, *when made with quality ingredients, is incredibly good ...*

SERVES 6 PREPARATION TIME: 10 MINUTES
COOKING TIME: 7 MINUTES

Place **3 organic eggs** in a saucepan of cold water and bring to the boil. Once it's boiling, time the eggs for 7 minutes so they are not too hard. Run the eggs under cold water and remove their shells, cut them in half and place **an anchovy** on each half with a toothpick. Scatter over a little **chopped parsley** and drizzle with **olive oil**.

SARDE FRITTE

FRIED SARDINES

Delicious and ubiquitous on the counters of the bàcari–wine bars–
these fried sardines are best hot but can also be eaten cold ...

<u>SERVES</u> 6 <u>PREPARATION TIME</u>: 30 MINUTES <u>COOKING TIME</u>: 5 MINUTES

12 small sardines
50 g (1¾ oz/⅓ cup) plain (all-purpose) flour
1 egg, beaten
50 g (1¾ oz) home-made breadcrumbs
1 litre (35 fl oz/4 cups) vegetable oil, for deep-frying

Cut the heads off the sardines and scale, clean and butterfly them. In a deep-fryer
or large heavy-based saucepan, heat the oil to 180°C (350°F), or until a cube of
bread dropped into the oil turns golden brown in 15 seconds. Put the flour, egg and
breadcrumbs in separate dishes. Dip the sardines first in the flour, shake off any
excess, then coat with the egg, and then the breadcrumbs. Fry them in the hot oil
until golden brown and drain on paper towels. Season with salt before serving.

<u>OVEN-BAKED VERSION</u>

Preheat the oven to 180°C (350°F/Gas 4). Lay the sardines on a baking tray lined
with baking paper. Sprinkle them with breadcrumbs and bake for 5 minutes.

CROSTINI, PANINI & TRAMEZZINI

A *panino* (plural *panini*) is a bread bun and a *crostino* (plural *crostini*) is a small slice of bread, about 1 cm (½ inch) thick, toasted or untoasted. They are usually filled or topped with local cured meats and cheeses, but also grilled vegetables, mozzarella or pesto, replaced by radicchio tardivo (see page 208) and *casatella* cheese in winter.

You absolutely must try: **baccalà mantecato** (see page 12) on a *crostino* of bread, a slice of grilled polenta or in a *piccolo panino*, and a tuna and horseradish *panino* (see page 22).

Don't miss out on the *crostini* served at All'Arco, unforgettable for their originality and the quality of their ingredients.

Tramezzini are small square or triangular sandwiches of soft crustless bread spread with a thin layer of mayonnaise or creamed butter and generously filled with a variety of ingredients, each tastier than the last. The combinations are endless …

PANINO
WITH TUNA & HORSERADISH

Al Mercà in the Rialto is the place to go in Venice to enjoy all sorts of panini ...

SERVES 6 PREPARATION TIME: 5 MINUTES

Grate **1 cm (½ inch) of horseradish root** into a bowl (or use 1 teaspoon horseradish cream, from an organic food store) and combine it with **2-3 tablespoons of mayonnaise**. Add **200 g (7 oz) tuna in oil**, drained and flaked, then process the mixture to a smooth cream. Split open **6 panini** and spread them with the tuna mixture.

VARIATION

In winter, add coarsely chopped radicchio tardivo (see page 208) to this *panino*.

CROSTINO
WITH CASATELLA & RADICCHIO TARDIVO

Classic Venice ingredients! If you can't find casatella, buy some stracchino or crescenza (delicious creamy cheeses and very similar to casatella) or a fresh, soft, rindless cheese.

SERVES 6 PREPARATION TIME: 20 MINUTES
COOKING TIME: 10 MINUTES

Wash **200 g (7 oz) radicchio tardivo** (see page 208) and cut into 2 cm (¾ inch) pieces. If you can't find radicchio tardivo, use English spinach or radish tops instead. Sauté on medium heat in a little **olive oil** with **1 garlic clove**, add **2½ tablespoons red wine** and cook for another 2 minutes, then add salt and pepper. Remove the garlic. Toast **6 slices of bread**. Spread **1 cm (½ inch) casatella** on the bread and add a small spoonful of sautéed radicchio. Season with pepper and drizzle with a little **truffle oil**, if you have it ...

CROSTINO

WITH CURED MEATS

Cured meats from the region can be enjoyed on a slice of toasted bread (a crostino). The local speciality is the prosciutto d'oca (goose ham), but there's also pancetta, sopressa trevigiana, which is a delicious soft salami … or the prosciuttos from San Daniele or Sauris, both in the neighbouring region of Friuli.

CROSTINO

WITH SMOKED TROUT & ASPARAGUS

This recipe is inspired by a very stylish crostino enjoyed at All'Arco, one of the best bàcari for cicheti in Venice. Trout is widely eaten in Veneto and the neighbouring region of Friuli.

SERVES 6 PREPARATION TIME: 10 MINUTES

Cut **4 fillets of smoked trout** into three sections. Lightly toast **12 slices of bread**, 1 cm (½ inch) thick. Let them cool, spread with butter and top with a piece of smoked trout, a **tip of blanched green asparagus** and a few **trout roe**.

TRAMEZZINO

WITH TUNA, EGG & TOMATO

SERVES 4 PREPARATION TIME: 10 MINUTES COOKING TIME: 12 MINUTES

2 eggs
200 g (7 oz) tuna in oil, drained and flaked
1-2 tablespoons mayonnaise
1 teaspoon chopped flat-leaf (Italian) parsley or basil
1 teaspoon salted capers, rinsed and chopped
4 slices of sandwich bread
2 small tomatoes, sliced

Place the eggs in a saucepan of cold water on medium heat. Time the eggs for
9 minutes once they come to the boil. When cool enough to handle shell them and
slice. Combine the tuna with the mayonnaise, parsley and capers. Spread 2 slices of
bread with the tuna mixture, top with 2 slices of egg and tomato. Top with the other
2 slices of bread. Hold down two opposite corners of the sandwich so the filling
stays in place, cut off the crusts and cut each sandwich in half to make triangles.

TRAMEZZINO

WITH ARTICHOKE & HAM

SERVES 4 PREPARATION TIME: 10 MINUTES

Drain **4–6 artichokes in oil** and slice them thinly. Spread a thin layer of **mayonnaise** or butter on **4 slices of sandwich bread**. Lay **a slice of ham** on 2 of the bread slices, then the artichoke. Top with the remaining 2 slices of bread. Hold down two opposite corners of the sandwich so the filling stays in place, cut off the crusts and cut each sandwich in half to make triangles.

TRAMEZZINO

WITH EGG & ANCHOVY

In Venice you can also find little tramezzini called francobollo, which literally means 'postage stamp'. This little sandwich that can also be called a quadrotto, meaning 'big square'.

MAKES 8 MINI SANDWICHES PREPARATION TIME: 15 MINUTES
COOKING TIME: 10 MINUTES

Place **3 eggs** in a saucepan of cold water on medium heat. Time the eggs for 7 minutes once they come to the boil to preserve their beautiful orange colour. Run them under cold water, remove the shells and cut into 1 cm (½ inch) slices. Chop **8 anchovy fillets**. Spread a thin layer of **mayonnaise** or butter on **4 slices of sandwich bread**. Arrange the boiled egg and anchovies on top of 2 slices of bread. Top with the remaining 2 slices. Hold down two opposite corners of the sandwich so the filling stays in place, cut off the crusts and cut each sandwich into four small squares.

PIERINO

CROQUE-MONSIEUR FROM HARRY'S BAR

*Pierino is the name given at Harry's Bar, the famous Venice
bar-restaurant, to this little rectangular toasted sandwich.
Here is the original recipe given to me by Arrigo Cipriani.*

MAKES 12 PIERINI (MINI TOASTED SANDWICHES)
PREPARATION TIME: 15 MINUTES COOKING TIME: 15 MINUTES

250 g (9 oz) emmental cheese, chopped
1 egg yolk
1 teaspoon worcestershire sauce
¼ teaspoon mustard
1 pinch of cayenne pepper
About 80 ml (2½ fl oz/⅓ cup) thin (pouring) cream
12 slices of good (artisan) sandwich bread (1 cm/½ inch thick)
110 g (3¾ oz) smoked ham (thinly sliced)
Olive oil, to fry

Put the cheese, egg yolk, worcestershire sauce, mustard and cayenne pepper
into a food processor, and process until you have a smooth mixture. Add
enough cream to make the mixture spreadable on the bread. Taste and
add salt if needed. Spread this cheese mixture on the 12 bread slices. Place
some ham on 1 slice of bread, top with another slice of bread and press
down firmly. Cut the crusts off the bread. Cut each sandwich in half. Heat a
frying pan and add a generous amount of olive oil. Brown the sandwiches
on both sides on medium heat, adding more oil if necessary. Serve hot.

MY RECOMMENDATIONS

This little toasted sandwich is very good if you use quality ingredients, starting with
the sandwich bread (get a loaf of fresh bread from the baker) and a good emmental
or young Comté cheese.

You can also brown the *pierini* in an oven preheated to 180°C (350°F/Gas 4), after
brushing them with oil.

FOLPETTI
MUSKY OCTOPUS

In the bàcari, these folpetti are served as aperitifs on toothpicks, accompanied by white wine. Folpetti is a Venetian term that means 'small octopus'. These small molluscs belong to the species Eledone moschata *that lives on the sandy sea bottom of the Adriatic. I especially love them served warm with pieces of celery. Thanks to Signora Mary Guadagnin (pictured) for her suggestions.*

SERVES 6 PREPARATION TIME: 20 MINUTES COOKING TIME: 15 MINUTES

12 musky octopus, or use 1.5 kg (3 lb 5 oz) small octopus
½ a lemon, plus the juice of 1 lemon
2 bay leaves
Black peppercorns
2 tablespoons olive oil
1 bunch of flat-leaf (Italian) parsley, chopped

Clean the octopus by removing the eyes, beak and internal cartilage with a knife. Clean out the insides well and wash them under running water. Bring a saucepan of water to the boil with the half lemon, bay leaves and a few peppercorns. Drop the octopus into the water, cover and cook for 15 minutes. Drain and allow to cool to room temperature. Dress with the oil, lemon juice and parsley, and season. Serve the octopus cut in half on small toothpicks.

NOTE

If you can't find musky octopus, use normal octopus and simmer or steam for about 15 minutes or more, depending on their size.

VARIATION: DEEP-FRIED OCTOPUS

This is a delicious way of cooking octopus when they are very small. Clean the octopus and wash well. In a deep-fryer or large heavy-based saucepan, heat 1 litre (35 fl oz/4 cups) of oil to 180°C (350°F), or until a cube of bread dropped into the oil turns golden brown in 15 seconds. Dip the octopus in plain (all-purpose) flour and deep-fry them until they are golden, then drain on paper towels. Season with salt and pepper and serve immediately with lemon wedges.

CANESTRELLI

BAKED QUEEN SCALLOPS

Canestrelli *(queen scallops)* are delicious little shellfish, almost sweet tasting and very common in Venetian cuisine. In former times, they were sold fresh from the lagoon in the streets and bàcari, where they were eaten raw in their shells … Scallops sold without their shells need to be cooked! Ask the fishmonger to open the shell and prepare them soon afterwards …

SERVES 6 PREPARATION TIME: 20 MINUTES COOKING TIME: 6 MINUTES

24 queen scallops in their shells, or scallops of choice
2 tablespoons home-made breadcrumbs
1 teaspoon chopped flat-leaf (Italian) parsley
Olive oil
Extra chopped herbs (e.g. flat-leaf (Italian) parsley, chives) to garnish (optional)

Preheat the oven to 180°C (350°F/Gas 4). Open each scallop shell by inserting the blade of an oyster knife between the two halves of the closed shell. Remove the scallop, wash it well to remove any sand and keep the shell. Place each scallop on a half shell and arrange them on a baking tray. Mix the breadcrumbs with the parsley and sprinkle over the scallops, add a drizzle of olive oil, season with salt and pepper and bake for 5-6 minutes. Remove from the oven and sprinkle with extra herbs if using. Serve with fresh bread to mop up the juices.

NOTE

To make the breadcrumbs, process a piece of dry bread in a food processor until you have breadcrumbs, not too fine. They can be flavoured with dried herbs such as rosemary or sage.

TIP

If you can't find scallops in the shell, serve in small dishes.

CALAMARI FARCITI SU POLENTA NERA

STUFFED SQUID ON BLACK POLENTA

*This is an original recipe inspired by the bàcaro Bancogiro in
the Rialto. The best lardo is from Colonnata or Arnad.*

SERVES 6 PREPARATION TIME: 40 MINUTES
COOKING TIME: 1 HOUR 20 MINUTES RESTING TIME: 1 HOUR

6 squid about 15 cm (6 inches) long, cleaned*
Olive oil
1 garlic clove, halved

THE STUFFING
6 potatoes
185 ml (6 fl oz/¾ cup) milk
Olive oil
2 thin slices of flavoured lardo, or pancetta, finely chopped
2 tablespoons chopped flat-leaf (Italian) parsley

THE BLACK POLENTA
1.4 litres (49 fl oz) water
350 g (12 oz) polenta (cornmeal)
1½ teaspoons salt
25 g (1 oz) cuttlefish or squid ink (available from the fishmonger)

To make the polenta: Bring the water to the boil, add salt, then add the polenta
in a stream and whisk for 2–3 minutes to prevent lumps from forming (follow
the instructions on the packet). Stir frequently. Cook for about 1 hour (or
according to packet instructions if you are using a quick-cooking polenta),
add the cuttlefish ink diluted in a little warm water and mix well to spread the
colour evenly. Pour the polenta into an oiled baking dish, 2 litre (70 fl oz/8 cup)
capacity, and let it cool completely (you can make it the day before). Cut
the polenta into 3–4 cm (1¼–1½ inch) squares about 1.5 cm (⅝ inch) thick.

To make the stuffing: Simmer the potatoes for 40 minutes, then peel. Heat the milk.
Mash the potatoes then incorporate the hot milk, stirring to make a purée. Add a
drizzle of olive oil, the lardo and the parsley. Taste before adding salt. Brown the
squid tentacles in a frying pan with a little olive oil on medium heat, season with
salt, then chop and add them to the purée. Stuff the squid tubes with this mixture.

Heat a little olive oil and the garlic in a frying pan on medium heat. When the
oil is hot, brown the stuffed calamari, turning them regularly so they don't
overcook, or they will become tough. Let them cool a little, cut them into
1 cm (½ inch) slices and serve them warm on the squares of black polenta.

VARIATION

If you can't find cuttlefish ink, normal polenta will work perfectly well.

* See page 80 for how to prepare squid.

PEPERONE E OMBRINA

CAPSICUM STUFFED WITH CREAMED UMBRINE

Umbrine is a highly prized fish with a delicate flesh that's common in the Venice lagoon and the Mediterranean.

SERVES 6 PREPARATION TIME: 30 MINUTES COOKING TIME: 15 MINUTES

1 x 600 g (1 lb 5 oz) umbrine, or use sea bass or hapuka
1 bay leaf
A few flat-leaf (Italian) parsley stalks
Mild olive oil
Zest of ½ an organic lemon
1 teaspoon chopped flat-leaf (Italian) parsley
6 small roasted capsicums (peppers), or piquillo peppers

Poach the fish in enough water to cover it with the bay leaf and parsley stalks on a very low simmer for about 15 minutes (or steam it). Flake the fish with your fingers and remove the bones. Put the fish in a food processor with a plastic blade or in an electric mixer with a paddle and beat as for a mayonnaise, adding the oil gradually until a smooth paste forms. Dress with the salt, pepper, lemon zest and parsley. Fill the capsicums with this mousse using two small spoons or a piping (icing) bag. Serve cold.

NOTE

This delicious recipe is inspired by a speciality of the Bancogiro restaurant in the Rialto neighbourhood.

TIP

If you don't have an electric mixer or food processor, put the fish into a fairly deep container, add the oil gradually and mix vigorously in the same direction with a wooden spoon until it is absorbed.

SALVIA FRITTA

FRIED SAGE

*My memories of fried sage are associated with rare
and special occasions: wedding buffets, birthdays …
It is delicious! When you are deep-frying at home,
take the opportunity to fry some sage as well.*

SERVES 6 PREPARATION TIME: 15 MINUTES
COOKING TIME: 10 MINUTES

Beat **1 egg**, mix in **100 g (3½ oz/⅔ cup) plain (all-purpose) flour**,
then blend in **250 ml (9 fl oz/1 cup) of cold mineral water** until you
have a batter that's smooth and quite dense (like a crepe batter). In
a fairly wide saucepan, heat **1 litre (35 fl oz/4 cups) of vegetable
oil** to 180°C (350°F), or until a cube of bread dropped into the
oil turns golden brown in 15 seconds. Dip **36 sage leaves** in the
batter, fry the leaves until they are golden on each side and drain
them on paper towels. Season with salt and serve immediately, or
keep them warm in an oven preheated to 120°C (235°F/Gas ½).

COTECHINO & POLENTA

COTECHINO & POLENTA

SERVES 6 PREPARATION TIME: 35 MINUTES

Place small thick slices of *cotechino* (see page 182) or
sopressa (local fresh sausage) on a slice of **polenta** that's
been browned for 20 minutes in the oven. Serve hot.

POLPETTE

MEATBALLS

*In Venice, don't miss the polpette fritte (deep-fried meatballs)
from the bàcaro-trattoria Cà D'Oro/Alla Vedova, located in a
little alleyway off the Strada Nuova, near the Cà D'Oro palace.
I took inspiration from it and give you a pan-fried version.*

SERVES 6 PREPARATION TIME: 30 MINUTES COOKING TIME: 10 MINUTES
RESTING TIME: 1 HOUR

80 g (2¾ oz) sandwich bread, crust removed
100 ml (3½ fl oz) milk
2 French shallots
10 g (¼ oz) butter
Olive oil
500 g (1 lb 2 oz) minced beef (15% fat)
2 tablespoons chopped flat-leaf (Italian) parsley
50 g (1¾ oz) parmesan cheese, grated
1 egg
Plain (all-purpose) flour, for dusting

Soak the bread in the milk before mashing it with a fork. Peel and chop the shallots
and sauté them in the butter and a little olive oil, then cool. Combine the minced
beef, bread, cooked shallots, parsley and parmesan in a mixing bowl, then add
the egg, salt and pepper. Shape the mixture into balls the size of a large walnut
in the palm of your hands. Dip them in the flour, place them on a dish, cover
with plastic wrap and let them firm up in the refrigerator for 1 hour. Brown the
meatballs in a little oil in a non-stick frying pan on medium heat, then reduce heat
and cook them gently for 10 minutes, turning regularly. Serve with toothpicks.

VARIATIONS

In a deep-fryer or large heavy-based saucepan, heat some oil to 180°C (350°F), or
until a cube of bread dropped into the oil turns golden brown in 15 seconds. Dip the
meatballs successively in flour, beaten egg and breadcrumbs to coat completely,
and deep-fry them in the oil. Brown them on all sides then drain on paper towels.
Let them cool a little before serving.

Instead of bread, mash 1–2 boiled potatoes. Once they have cooled, mix them with
the minced beef.

You can also use minced cooked beef—the leftovers from a *bollito misto* (see
page 180)—and mix it with a little chopped mortadella and an egg. If the mixture is
too soft, add some flour or breadcrumbs.

FRITTATA DI ERBE

GREEN FRITTATA

In Veneto, this frittata is served with drinks, quite thick and cut
into pieces. It is made with all kinds of vegetables, cured meats or
cheeses. In former times, cooks had a wide cast-iron frying pan with a
thick and perfectly flat base which they used only for frittatas. They
never washed it, just wiped it clean with a cloth after each use.

SERVES 6 PREPARATION TIME: 15 MINUTES
COOKING TIME: 20 MINUTES

Olive oil
3 silverbeet (Swiss chard) leaves, shredded
200 g (7 oz) English spinach, shredded
1 leek, green part only, shredded
1 onion, thinly sliced
A few basil leaves
3 sage leaves
8 eggs

Heat a heavy-based frying pan with a little olive oil, add the silverbeet,
spinach, leek, onion, basil and sage, and cook on medium heat for 10 minutes, stirring
frequently. Cool slightly. Break the eggs into a bowl and beat them with a little
salt and pepper. Add the green vegetables to the eggs and mix well. Heat a little
more oil in the frying pan on high heat. Pour in the egg-vegetable mixture. When
the eggs start to stick on the side, bring them towards the centre with a wooden
spatula. Once the bottom has set, place a large plate on top of the frying pan
and quickly turn over the frittata. Add a little more oil to the frying pan and
slide the frittata back into the pan to brown the other side. Serve hot or cold.

NOTE

The omelette should be cooked on high heat so the beaten eggs form a golden
crust on the outside and are creamy inside.

VARIATIONS

Here are a few frittata ideas:

• *rognosa:* with onion and smoked bacon, diced

• *luganega:* with crumbled sausage meat

• with boiled prawns

• with *bruscandoli* (wild hop shoots), blanched briefly

• with chopped asparagus

CORNETTO DI FRITTURA DI PESCE

FRIED SEAFOOD CONE

In Venice, mixed fried seafood served as an aperitif often contains small cuttlefish, squid, prawns, small oily fish (sardines, anchovies ...), scallops and scampi ... It's a real luxury. I enjoyed this exquisite fried seafood cone at the restaurant Antiche Carampane, which I thank for its good advice.

SERVES 6 PREPARATION TIME: 30 MINUTES
COOKING TIME: 20 MINUTES RESTING TIME: 15 MINUTES

300 g (10½ oz) scampi tails (langoustines, red-claw crayfish or large prawns/shrimp)
6 raw gamba prawns (shrimp), or other large variety of your choosing
6 small squid
300 g (10½ oz) small frying fish
300 g (10½ oz) scallops
Plain (all-purpose) flour
1 litre (35 fl oz/4 cups) vegetable oil, for deep-frying
Lemon wedges to serve

Shell the scampi tails and prawns. Clean the squid by removing their insides and cartilage, rinse them well and slice into rings. Wash the fish well. Place the prawns, scampi, squid, fish and scallops in iced cold water and let them chill. Toss the seafood in the flour, tapping off any excess. In a deep-fryer or large heavy-based saucepan, heat the oil to 180°C (350°F), or until a cube of bread dropped into the oil turns golden brown in 15 seconds. Fry the biggest fish until golden brown, then fry the smaller ones. Drain on paper towels. Repeat the process with the squid, prawns and scallops. Place the seafood in paper cones specially made for fried food, season with salt and serve immediately with lemon wedges.

VARIATION

If you replace the flour with polenta (cornmeal), it gives a slightly different taste and, because it is not as fine as flour, it is also crispier.

NOTE

It's the thermal shock between the icy-cold fish and the hot cooking oil that gives lightness to the dish.

SESTRIERE - CANNAREGIO

FROM THE PONTE DELLE GUGLIE ACROSS THE GHETTO

From the station, turn left into the Lista di Spagna, and already there's a first chance to indulge at the **Pasticceria Dal Mas (1)** which dates back to 1853. At the counter, order an espresso or a *caffè d'orzo macchiato* (a barley-based 'coffee' with a small amount of milk froth served in a small or large cup) and take away some typical Venetian cakes (*focaccia, zaletti, esse, bucellati, pan dei dogi, torta veneziana ...*) with you.

Once past the Ponte delle Guglie, turn left towards Il Ghetto (the Jewish quarter). A brief stop at **Panificio Giovanni Volpi (2)** (Volpi bakery), which makes matzo crackers and traditional certified Kosher biscuits (no salt, yeast or animal fats). Try the *azimo dolce* with fennel seeds and the round *zuccherino*. In the central square of the Ghetto, called the 'Campo del Ghetto Nuovo', you can visit the Jewish museum and the synagogues.

For an aperitif, leave the square via the bridge and turn right onto the Fondamenta degli Ormesini. You will find **Al Timon (3)** (part of Venice's nightlife takes place in this Fondamenta, as well as in the Fondamenta Misericordia). Take advantage of the tables placed outside when the weather is fine. At the counter you will find a good selection of *cicheti*. If you decide to sit down at a table, you should know that this is one of the rare places in Venice that sells chargrilled meat.

For a simple and economical lunch, turn left after the Ghetto bridge into the Fondamenta delle Cappucine, far from the tourist flow. In this working-class neighbourhood, don't miss the **Alle due gondolette (4)** restaurant, which serves more than respectable family cooking. Try the *baccalà mantecato* or the *baccalà alla vicentina*.

Continue your promenade to the right, towards the Campo dei Mori (don't miss the statues of eighteenth-century merchants).

For dinner, let me take you to a very enjoyable spot ... On the Fondamenta degli Ormesini, take the Calle de la Malvasia. After the little bridge, you will find **Anice Stellato (5)** on the right. When the weather is fine, you can eat outside in total tranquillity. The restaurant is also very pleasant inside. Franca, the chef, and her team will take very good care of you. The menu changes every day. You have to try the *frittura* of fish and vegetables! At night, you can enjoy a last drink in one of the bars of the Fondamenta della Misericordia.

FROM THE PONTE DELLE GUGLIE TO THE STRADA NUOVA.

At the Ponte delle Guglie, go straight ahead down Rio Terrà San Leonardo. You will go past the fruit and vegetable stalls of the market in Campo San Leonardo. After you've done your shopping, have a quick coffee in one of the last *torrefaziones* (coffee roasters) in Venice: **Torrefazione Marchi (6)**. Try the *caffè della Sposa* (made with one of the best arabica beans), or buy 200 g (7 oz) freshly ground costarica. Continue on to the Strada Nuova. Stop in the Campo San Felice. With its outside tables, **La Cantina (7)** ('the cellar') alone is worth a stop whatever the time of day. As its name suggests, it's a place to drink good wine, but also a house beer, Morgana. Let Francesco advise you. He prepares high quality, market-driven dishes such as his plate of raw and cooked fish with crisp seasonal vegetables.

Cross the street opposite La Cantina towards the Fondamenta San Felice, where you should eat at least once at **Vini Da Gigio (8)**. This little restaurant of exceptional quality is my latest crush. It offers traditional dishes with great freshness. Laura has taken over from her mother in the kitchen. Her brother Paolo will advise you on wines. The restaurant houses a cellar that's well stocked with both local wines and wines from elsewhere. Try their *grappa* as well. On the food front, I suggest you try ... everything! Still, don't miss the *baccalà* croquettes, the roast eel or the duck *alla buranella* (served in autumn and winter). Make sure you book in advance. It is easier to find a seat at **Antica Adelaide (9)**, a larger and simpler restaurant in the same neighbourhood. It's an 'historic tavern' (*osteria antica*). To find it, cross the Nuovo San Felice bridge and turn left, then left again after the Campo and follow the Calle Priuli. The young owner and chef Alvise serves very honest local cuisine. I loved his *tagliatelle al ragù di castrato* (mutton), which reminded me of my grandmother's.

Returning back up the Strada Nuova, just opposite the yellow sign for the Cà D'Oro palace, in the little Calle del Pistor alleyway, is a historic and picturesque *bàcaro-trattoria* that has two names: **Alla Vedova** and **Cà D'Oro (10)**. This is a real institution. People jostle at the counter to get to its *cicheti* (mouthfuls to eat with drinks). Try the meatballs, the artichoke hearts and the sardines *in saor*. Remember that while *cicheti* are enjoyed as a bite with drinks, they can also play the role of lunch or dinner. At the nearby Campo Santa Sofia, take the gondola to the opposite bank, which is to say to the Rialto where there's a market in the morning. (fare: €2 per person for non-residents). Be careful not to fall into the water!

Fond. dei Riformati
C. d. Riformati
C. Contarina
C. d. Squero
C. Cappuccine

C. del Capitel
C. d. Rotur
C. longa Canossia

CANNAREGIO

Fond. della

C. d. Malvasia

5

C. d. Muneghe

Sensa

C. DI S. ALVISE

Fond. Madonna dell'Orto

C. larga Piave

Fond. Gasparo Contarini

C. Loredan
C. Fond.
dei C. Mori
C. Brazzo

C. DEI MORI

3

Fondamenta degli

C. d. Forno

Ormesini

Fond. della Misericordia

C. Larga

Corte Vecchia

Fond. dell'Abbazia

C. d. Zoccolo

C. larga Lezze

CAMPO GHETTO NUOVO

C. Farnese

C. Selle

C. della Masena

Rio terrà Farsetti

Calle dell'Aseo

Fond. Canal

Fond. Moro

Fond. Diedo

C. Zancani

Fond. Trapolin

Calle del Ghetto Vecchio
d. Forno

2

6

PONTE D. GUGLIE

Rio terrà San Leonardo

C. S. LEONARDO

C. d. Chiesa

C. Colonna

C. Querini

R. terrà dietro la Chiesa

R. terrà della Maddalena

C. larga Vendramin

CAMPIELLO DE LA CHIESA

C. STA FOSCA

Via V. Emanuele

Calle della Racchetta

8

Calle San Felice

C. larga Doge Priuli

9

C. Corrente

CAMPO EREMIA

Fond. Labia

7

Strada

10

Nova

C. STA SOFIA

C. d. Forno

di Biasio

Riva

Rio Terrà

Calle e Ramo Zen

Fondaco dei Turchi

C. del Megio

C. del Forno

Sal. San Stae

C. SAN STAE

C. SAN STAE

Fond. rimpetto Mocenigo

Fond. Ca Pesaro

C. Corner

C. del Ravano

C. d. Rosa

Fond. dell'Olio

CAMPO DELLA PESCARIA

Lista dei Bari

C. Pisani

Ramo Cazza

C. Gallion

C. larga dei Bari

C. del Tentor

C. Colombo

Fond. delle Grue

C. della Chiesa

C. della Regina

CAMPO S. CASSIANO

Botteri

CAMPO BECCARIE

R. degli Speziali

CAMPO NAZARIO SAURO

Ruga Bella

C. SAN GIACOMO DELL'ORIO

C. del Tintor

C. Cristi

C. dei

C. S. Mattio

R. Due Mori

vecch. S. Giov.

R. d.

C. SAN GIACOMETO

Rio Marin o Garzotti

CAMPO DELLE STROPE

C. delle Oche

C. DI S. AGOSTIN

R. terrà Secondo

C. del Cristo

C. dell' Agnello

Rio terrà delle Carampane

C. Raspi

C. Sansoni

Orefici

Rio Marin

Visciga

Calle Zane

C. della Chiesa

C. Scaleter

C. Bernardo

C. Pezzana

SAN POLO

C. S. APONAL

Rugheta del Ravano

Ruga

C. d. Madonna

C. dei Cinque

C. del Storione

Vin

CAMPO

C. Cor...

OMBRA DI VINO

'Andemo bever un ombra!', literally 'let's go drink a shadow'. This very old Venetian expression means 'let's go have a glass of wine'. It derives from the bell tower of San Marco. In paintings from the fourteenth century, you can see a number of stalls at the base of the tower, including those of wine merchants. To keep their wine cool, they moved their stall around the tower, following the shadow with the movement of the sun. The shadow ended up meaning the wine itself and Venetians started talking about going to drink a 'shadow'. The expression persists to this day. To be even more precise, an *ombra* means exactly one decilitre (100 ml/3½ fl oz) of wine.

BELLINI

SERVES 1 PREPARATION TIME: 15 MINUTES

The Bellini is a cocktail that's known worldwide. It was invented in 1930 by Giuseppe Cipriani at Harry's Bar in Venice. But it was only in 1948, at the time of an exhibition of fifteenth-century Venetian painters in which the artist Bellini featured prominently, that Cipriani baptised it the 'Bellini' in his honour. Arrigo Cipriani, the son of Giuseppe, gave us his recipe. He explained that previously the Bellini was only served during peach season, whereas today it is enjoyed at any time of year thanks to the freezer. White peaches are puréed with their skin and strained through a chinois or food mill, not blended in a food-processor or the purée fills with air. It is mixed with a good prosecco from Conegliano or a good spumante (sparkling wine). Measure three parts prosecco to one part peach juice, nothing else!

SPRITZ

The spritz is the most common aperitif in Venice and Veneto. In recent years, its popularity has spread to the whole of Italy and even beyond. The colour of a spritz varies from orange to red and amber. You can't miss them in the bars. Its name comes from the Austrian language: during the Austrian domination of Venice in the late eighteenth century, the occupiers were in the habit of squirting–'spritzen' in German–extra water into their white wine. Today, we refer to a spritz liscio for a white wine with added sparkling water and spritz aperol, spritz campari or spritz bitter when Aperol, Campari, Select or Ramazzotti Aperitivo are added, according to taste. Drink in moderation! Excessive alcohol intake is dangerous to your health!

Ice cubes
2 parts Aperol, Campari, Select or the new Ramazzotti Aperitivo
3 parts white wine, or prosecco
1 part sparkling mineral water
1 slice orange
1 olive

Put a handful of ice cubes in a large glass, add the alcohol of your choice, white wine and sparkling water (add more for a lighter spritz). Mix well, add the slice of orange and the olive on a cocktail stick and serve. Have a *cicheto* with your spritz: a little something to nibble on.

ANTIPASTI

APPETISERS

ANTIPASTO

OF RAW FISH

This recipe, inspired by a magnificent dish I enjoyed at the restaurant Antiche Carampane, demands extra fresh fish. If you are in Venice, buy your fish from Marco Bergamasco in the Rialto fish market. Marco only sells excellent pescato, which is to say fish from the lagoon and the Adriatic. You will not find Mediterranean tuna on his stall (which is only allowed to be fished at certain times of the year), but Marco will tell you where to find it. Otherwise, ask for advice from your usual fishmonger.

SERVES 6 PREPARATION TIME: 30 MINUTES

500 g (1 lb 2 oz) umbrine, or use sea bream or other firm white fish
500 g (1 lb 2 oz) sea bass, or use hapuka or barramundi
250 g (9 oz) fresh tuna
6 live scampi (langoustines, red-claw crayfish or large prawns/shrimp)–if they
    are still alive when you get home, put them in the freezer for 10 minutes
½ a pomegranate
Mild olive oil
Juice of 1 lemon
Fleur de sel (fine sea salt)
1½ tablespoons horseradish cream, or 1 tablespoon grated
    horseradish root, mixed with mascarpone cheese
1 teaspoon chopped flat-leaf (Italian) parsley

Ask the fishmonger to fillet the fish. Slice thinly. Arrange a few slices of each fish and a shelled scampi on each plate. Remove the seeds from the pomegranate. Dress the fish with a little olive oil and a dash of lemon juice, season with salt and pepper. Scatter the pomegranate seeds over the fish, the horseradish cream on the tuna, and sprinkle with the parsley.

RECOMMENDATION

To make the fish easier to slice, place it in the freezer for about 10 minutes beforehand.

NOTE

Horseradish is a pungent root with digestive properties from the same family as the Japanese wasabi. It is called *rafano* in Italy. In Veneto, it's called *cren*. It has been widely used from the time of the Austrian occupation of Venice in the late eighteenth century, especially with ham and *bollito* (see page 180). Grated horseradish root (fresh or canned) is used, or horseradish sauce.

ANTIPASTO ALLA VENEZIANA

VENETIAN-STYLE ANTIPASTO

This combination is inspired by a very delicious and typical antipasti dish enjoyed at the restaurant Antiche Carampane. Choose your own antipasti (from this chapter) based on the season and what's at the market.

SERVES 6 PREPARATION TIME: 45 MINUTES COOKING TIME: 30 MINUTES

300 g (10½ oz) *baccalà mantecato* (see page 12)
20 raw mantis prawns (shrimp) (see note below)
3 lemons
Olive oil
1 bunch of flat-leaf (Italian) parsley (½ chopped and ½ left whole)
600 g (1 lb 5 oz) octopus, cleaned*
1 garlic clove, crushed
300 g (10½ oz) small raw school prawns (shrimp)
½ cup cooked soft polenta (cornmeal), or 6 slices of toast
300 g (10½ oz) monkfish cheeks, or use flathead or stargazer
3 tablespoons tomato passata (puréed tomatoes), or crushed tomato

All the ingredients are cooked separately, some steamed, others pan-fried. Wash the prawns, blanch them in boiling water and then simmer gently in water with salt, pepper and half a lemon for 3–5 minutes, depending on their size. Drain and let them cool slightly. Remove their shell by cutting along the sides (lengthways) with a pair of scissors. Extract the meat, then drizzle with olive oil, a little salt, pepper and lemon juice. Sprinkle with chopped parsley. Steam the octopus for 15 minutes or more depending on its size (it's cooked when it's tender). Drain and drizzle with olive oil, lemon juice, a little chopped parsley and garlic. Shell the school prawns (small ones can also be eaten with their shell). Pan-fry them for 2 minutes in a little olive oil on medium heat, season them with salt and place on some hot polenta. Pan-fry the monkfish cheeks in a little olive oil on medium heat for 3–4 minutes, add the passata, and sprinkle with a little chopped parsley at the end of the cooking time. Season with salt and pepper. Place them on some hot polenta.

Purée the leaves of the unchopped parsley with a little olive oil, the juice and zest of a lemon, salt and pepper. Arrange the different kinds of seafood on large plates. Serve with a small spoonful of parsley oil.

RECOMMENDATION

Ask the fishmonger if the octopus has been frozen. If not, freeze it and thaw it by steaming it, it will be even more tender!

NOTE

Mantis prawns, called *canoce* in Venetian, are also known as 'squilles' in French. You can substitute with another large prawn.

* See page 32 for how to prepare octopus.

CARPACCIO

SERVED CIPRIANI STYLE

In the 1950s, Giuseppe Cipriani, the owner of the legendary Harry's Bar in Venice, served thin slices of raw beef to a female customer who was no longer supposed to eat cooked meat. He baptised his dish 'carpaccio' in honour of the Venetian painter of the same name who was the subject of a retrospective in Venice at the time, some of whose reds were reminiscent of raw beef. This is the recipe kindly given to me by Arrigo Cipriani, Giuseppe's son.

<u>SERVES</u> 6 <u>PREPARATION TIME:</u> 30 MINUTES

1.3 kg (3 lb) beef sirloin (equivalent to about 650 g/1 lb 7 oz trimmed)
Fleur de sel (fine sea salt)

THE DRESSING

Home-made mayonnaise (made with 1 squeeze lemon juice, 2 egg yolks, 1 teaspoon
    mustard and 150 ml (5 fl oz) mild olive oil or grapeseed oil), or ready-made mayonnaise.
1 teaspoon fresh lemon juice
1-2 teaspoons worcestershire sauce
2-3 tablespoons milk

To make the mayonnaise: Dissolve two pinches of salt and pepper in a squeeze of lemon juice and mix in the egg yolks, then the mustard and, adding the oil in a thin stream, whisk to an emulsion. Add the lemon juice, worcestershire sauce and milk to the mayonnaise to make a pouring sauce. Check the seasoning.

Remove the fat and sinew from the beef and trim to a cylindrical shape, then refrigerate for 15 minutes. Cut the meat into very thin slices using a very sharp knife and arrange them on six plates. Season with salt, cover with plastic wrap and set aside in the refrigerator for a maximum of 2 hours. To serve, drizzle the meat with streaks of sauce as if you were creating an abstract painting–'Kandinsky-style', in the words of Arrigo Cipriani.

MY VARIATIONS

I like to add a vegetable touch to this dish: a few pieces of radicchio tardivo (see page 208) for crunch in the mouth, or some rocket and a little lemon zest.

TIP

Arrigo Cipriani recommends using beef sirloin, which is a very flavoursome cut, and placing the meat in the refrigerator for 15 minutes so it is easier to slice (but above all don't freeze it). You can also ask your butcher to cut the meat on a slicer. In that case, I suggest you bring him the serving dish so he can place the meat directly on it. Alternatively, make thin slices by placing 4-5 slices of meat between two sheets of baking paper and flattening them with a meat tenderiser or saucepan.

GRANSEOLA ALLA VENEZIANA

VENETIAN-STYLE SPIDER CRAB

Spider crab is an unmissable antipasto dish in Venetian cuisine, a luxury you mustn't deny yourself. It is served simply dressed with a drizzle of mildly flavoured olive oil, a squeeze of lemon and a hint of parsley, which showcases its delicate and tasty flesh. This large crustacean is found in the Mediterranean and Adriatic. Choose small spider crabs, weighing 250 g–300 g (9 oz–10½ oz). They're more delicate than the large ones and better suited to an antipasto course. The recipe is simple, you just need time and patience!

SERVES 6 PREPARATION TIME: 1½ HOURS COOKING TIME: 20 MINUTES

½ a lemon plus the juice of 3 lemons
Peppercorns
6 live spider crabs, or crab of your choice
Mild olive oil
A few flat-leaf (Italian) parsley sprigs, chopped

Place crabs in the freezer for 30 minutes to put to sleep. Bring a large saucepan of water to the boil with the half lemon, a few peppercorns and some salt. Drop in the spider crabs. Cook for 20 minutes on a very gentle simmer, then leave them to cool in the cooking liquid. Drain the crabs. Detach the legs and claws and crack them with a nutcracker. Remove the meat with a crab fork and set aside. Open up the shell by cutting into the ventral section, extract the gills, then remove the roe and place in a bowl. Take out the coral and place it in another container. Carefully remove the meat and cut it into small pieces, using a crab fork for the difficult parts, and making sure to separate hard parts and remove any cartilage. Set the flesh aside together with the coral and the meat from the claws and legs. Mix together the roe and the creamy brownish part of the spider crab in another bowl and season with salt and pepper. Drizzle the meat and coral with olive oil and add salt, pepper, a little lemon juice and parsley. Mix together gently then place in the emptied and cleaned shells. Serve with the roe mixture. Enjoy at room temperature.

CAPESANTE AL FORNO

BAKED SAINT JAMES SCALLOPS

This is one of the specialities of Venetian cuisine. The best time to eat scallops in Venice is from September to May. The ones caught in Venice are exquisite!

SERVES 6 PREPARATION TIME: 20 MINUTES COOKING TIME: 10 MINUTES

12 scallops in half shells
2 tablespoons finely chopped flat-leaf (Italian) parsley
3 tablespoons olive oil
½ a garlic clove, crushed
125 ml (4 fl oz/½ cup) white wine (optional)
3 tablespoons home-made breadcrumbs

Clean empty scallop shells and reserve. Clean the scallops just before cooking by removing any tough sinew and dark parts. Pat them dry with paper towels. Preheat the oven to 200°C (400°F/Gas 6). Make a sauce from the parsley, olive oil, salt, pepper and a touch of garlic and gently toss with the scallops, including the coral. Pour a little white wine in the bottom of each shell, add a scallop with sauce, sprinkle with breadcrumbs and bake for 10 minutes, then serve.

TIP FROM CHEF LAURA FROM THE RESTAURANT VINI DA GIGIO

Make the breadcrumbs ahead of time so they have more flavour. You can add a little crushed garlic and some dried herbs, such as rosemary, sage and thyme.

LE CAPELONGHE

VENETIAN-STYLE RAZOR CLAMS

Razor clams or capelonghe (pronounced 'cap-eh-longay') in Venetian, cannolicchi in Italian, are typical shellfish of the Venice lagoon. I love their almost sweet flavour. To prepare them properly, disgorge them in salted water for at least 2 hours because they can contain sand. For the same reason, I don't recommend eating the blackish pouch at one end of the clam, which is filled with sand. Keep a close eye on the razor clams as they cook. As soon as they open from the heat, they are ready. They become rubbery if they are overcooked.

SERVES 6 SOAKING TIME: 2 HOURS PREPARATION TIME : 15 MINUTES
COOKING TIME: 10 MINUTES

1.5 kg (3 lb 5 oz) razor clams
2 handfuls of coarse salt
2–3 tablespoons mild olive oil
Freshly ground black pepper
2 tablespoons chopped flat-leaf (Italian) parsley

Wash the razor clams well and soak them in a basin of cold water with the coarse salt for 2 hours to disgorge their sand. Heat a grill pan on high heat. When it is quite hot, place the razor clams on it. As soon as they open, remove them from the pan. Strain the cooking juices through a fine sieve to remove any residual sand. Combine the strained liquid with the olive oil, 2 turns of the pepper mill and 1 teaspoon of parsley. Check whether you need to add salt. Serve the razor clams hot, sprinkled with the remaining parsley and the olive oil dressing.

OVEN-BAKED VERSION

Preheat the oven to 220°C (425°F/Gas 7) and cook the razor clams dry on a tray until the shells open, then dress them the same way.

CANOCE BOLLITE

VENETIAN-STYLE MANTIS PRAWNS

Mantis prawns, canoce in Venetian (pronounced 'can-o-chay'), cannocchia in Italian, are crustaceans from the Adriatic that are highly appreciated in Veneto. A proverb of the lagoon fishermen goes: 'On the feast of Saint Catherine, a cannocchia is worth a chicken'. A cannocchia is worth a great deal then, especially as the feast day of Saint Catherine falls in late November, the best season for enjoying 'cannocchie'! That's when they are meaty and firm, packed with coral. They must be bought live. To appreciate the full delicacy of their flesh, they are dressed very simply with a drizzle of a light olive oil (preferably from Lake Garda or Liguaria), a squeeze of lemon juice and lightly sprinkled with parsley. This recipe is very simple, but it requires patience and a good pair of scissors. Watch out, mantis prawn tails can prick!

<u>SERVES</u> 6 <u>PREPARATION TIME:</u> 20 MINUTES <u>COOKING TIME:</u> 15 MINUTES

1.5 kg (3 lb 5 oz) live mantis prawns (shrimp), or large raw variety of your choosing
½ a lemon
A few peppercorns
3 tablespoons mild olive oil
A few flat-leaf (Italian) parsley sprigs, chopped
Freshly ground black pepper

Wash the prawns thoroughly. Bring a large saucepan of water to the boil with the lemon and peppercorns. Lightly salt the water and add the prawns. Simmer for 5 minutes then drain. Shell the mantis prawns by cutting down the sides of the body between head and tail with scissors. Drizzle with olive oil, and sprinkle with chopped parsley and a little pepper to serve.

VARIATION

Steam the mantis prawns for about 10 minutes.

MAZZANCOLLE IN PADELLA

PAN-FRIED CARAMOTE PRAWNS

Mazzancolle (caramote prawns) are large prawns that are typical of the Venice lagoon. Venetian mazzancolle are especially delicious. When I am in Veneto, I take the opportunity to enjoy them pan-fried or simply boiled and dressed with olive oil, lemon juice and parsley, served as a salad with radicchio tardivo (see page 208) and pomegranate.

SERVES 6 PREPARATION TIME: 40 MINUTES COOKING TIME: 10 MINUTES

24 raw caramote prawns (shrimp), or large variety of your choosing
6 small purple artichokes (if unavailable use green)
3 tablespoons olive oil
1 tablespoon chopped flat-leaf (Italian) parsley
50 g (1¾ oz) rocket leaves

Shell the prawns: Leave the head on and cut along the back to remove the intestine that looks like a black thread. Clean the artichokes and discard the outer leaves. Slice them very thinly. Heat 2 tablespoons of oil in a frying pan on low heat and sauté the artichoke for 5 minutes: they need to stay *al dente*. Remove the slices of artichoke from the pan, increase the heat to medium, add the remaining oil and the prawns and cook for 1 minute on each side. Return the artichoke to the pan and sauté for another minute. Sprinkle with chopped parsley and lightly season with salt and pepper. Serve with rocket.

VARIATION FROM THE TRATTORIA ALTANELLA

Once the prawns are cooked, add some balsamic vinegar to the pan and boil, stirring, for 30 seconds to deglaze the pan then add the artichoke and parsley.

MO'ECHE FRITTE

DEEP-FRIED SOFT-SHELL CRABS

Two kinds of small crabs are eaten in Venice, mo'eche and masanete. They are sold live and they're easy to spot at the market because they won't stay still! The mo'eche (pronounced 'moe-ekkeh') are the males, from the lagoon. During the moulting period (autumn and spring), they lose their shell and become soft. They are eaten deep-fried, just dipped in flour or 'stuffed', as in the recipe below. You eat them whole! Note that only 10%–15% of farmed crabs become mo'eche. This is why this rare dish is fairly expensive.

SERVES 6 PREPARATION TIME: 15 MINUTES
COOKING TIME: 15 MINUTES RESTING TIME: 2 HOURS

800 g (1 lb 12 oz) *mo'eche* (small soft-shell crabs)
4 eggs
50 g (1¾ oz) parmesan cheese, grated
Plain (all-purpose) flour
1 litre (35 fl oz/4 cups) vegetable oil, for deep-frying

Wash the crabs well several times under running water. In a mixing bowl, beat the eggs with the grated parmesan and add a pinch of salt. Add the crabs to the mix, stirring to coat well. Heat the oil in a deep-fryer or large heavy-based saucepan to 180°C (350°F), or until a cube of bread dropped into the oil turns golden brown in 15 seconds. Drain the crabs, dip them in flour and deep-fry until they're golden brown. Enjoy. It's a good idea to remove the ends of their claws, which are less digestible, although almost nobody does!

VARIATION

The Venetians call the female *mo'eche masanete*. Autumn is the perfect season to eat them because it's the moulting period and they're full of coral. They aren't eaten deep-fried like *mo'eche*, but boiled for 7 minutes and cooled in their cooking liquid. You need to remove their legs and abdominal wall. They're dressed with olive oil and parsley and served with polenta.

NOTE

In Venice this recipe would be made with live crabs and after washing the crabs and making the egg and parmesan mixture as described above, you would submerge the crabs in the mixture, cover the bowl with a lid (or they'll escape!), and leave for 2 hours, stirring occasionally. The crabs will eat the egg mixture until they 'drown' in it.

CHELE DI GRANSOPORRO AL ROSMARINO

CRAB CLAWS WITH ROSEMARY

An easy and very tasty recipe for crab claws. These are most often found at the market in autumn or winter, although spring is the best season to fully appreciate their meat.

SERVES 6 PREPARATION TIME: 15 MINUTES COOKING TIME: 15 MINUTES

12 raw crab claws
4 rosemary stalks
1 bay leaf
A few pieces of lemon zest
2 handfuls of coarse salt
2 garlic cloves, halved
80 ml (2½ fl oz/⅓ cup) olive oil

Wash the claws under cold running water. Bring a large quantity of water to the boil in a large saucepan with 2 of the rosemary stalks, the bay leaf, lemon zest and salt. Drop in the claws and cook for 7 minutes. Crack the claws with a nutcracker. Sauté the garlic and the rest of the rosemary in the olive oil in a frying pan on low heat. Increase the heat to medium, add the claws and stir for 3 minutes so they soak up all the flavours. Remove the garlic. Using a crab fork, remove the meat from the claws and serve hot.

VARIATIONS

Combine the creamy parts of the crab with lemon juice, olive oil, parsley, salt and freshly ground black pepper. Return the crab meat to the cleaned shells and serve with the sauce and pieces of toast.

For Venetian-style *gransoporro* (dressed with oil and a squeeze of lemon juice), use whole crabs and cook them in a court-bouillon like the spider crabs (see page 62). To open up the crab once it's cooked, lay it on its back, remove the claws and legs and then open it up like a box by pressing on the side towards the eyes. Remove the creamy brown meat with a spoon. Split the shell in half to remove the white meat. Crack the legs and claws and carefully remove their meat.

FRUTTI DI MARE SALTATI

SAUTÉED SHELLFISH

This shellfish dish is a feast, made with whatever is freshest according to the season and cooked the same day to make the most of its freshness.

SERVES 6 SOAKING TIME: 2 HOURS PREPARATION TIME: 20 MINUTES
COOKING TIME: 15 MINUTES

500 g (1 lb 2 oz) mussels
500 g (1 lb 2 oz) scallops in their shells (200 g/7 oz without their shells)
500 g (1 lb 2 oz) cockles or venus clams
500 g (1 lb 2 oz) carpet shell clams, or other clams
Coarse salt
3 tablespoons olive oil
1 garlic clove, halved
1 teaspoon chopped flat-leaf (Italian) parsley
100 ml (3½ fl oz) white wine
A few slices of good bread

Scrub the mussels, pulling out their hairy beards, and carefully clean the other shellfish. Soak them for at least 2 hours in water with the coarse salt so they disgorge their sand. Heat the oil in a deep frying pan with the garlic and parsley on medium heat. After a few minutes, add the white wine, wait for the liquid to come to the boil, then add the different shellfish separately. Cover. As soon as the shells have opened, remove and place in a bowl. Discard any broken or closed shellfish. Strain the cooking juices. Serve the shellfish with the combined cooking juices and good bread to mop them up!

VARIATION

The *osteria* Alle Testiere, which serves food that's traditional and innovative at the same time, adds grated ginger to this dish, giving a pleasant, exotic touch. They also use sweet spices in their dishes, as was common practice when Venice, at its peak, dominated maritime trade.

SARDE IN SAOR

SWEET & SOUR SARDINES

The saor ('flavour') is a marinade whose main ingredient is onion. It dates back to the fourteenth century. The tradition today in Venice is to make sarde in saor to eat on board boats during the great Festa del Redentore (Festival of the Redeemer) on the third Saturday in July, but they can be found throughout the year in the bàcari and in restaurants as a starter.

SERVES 6 PREPARATION TIME: 45 MINUTES COOKING TIME: 20 MINUTES
RESTING TIME: AT LEAST 24 HOURS

185 ml (6 fl oz/¾ cup) olive oil
500 g (1 lb 2 oz) white onions, thinly sliced
375 ml (13 fl oz/1½ cups) white vinegar
1 kg (2 lb 4 oz) fresh sardines
1 litre (35 fl oz/4 cups) vegetable oil, for deep-frying
Plain (all-purpose) flour
A few currants (optional, see note below)
A few pine nuts (optional, see note below)
Ground cinnamon (optional, see note below)

Heat the olive oil in a large non-stick frying pan. Add the onion and cook it on low heat until it is translucent. Add the vinegar and cook for 5 minutes, then remove from heat. Clean the sardines, removing their heads and insides and dry them on paper towels. In a deep-fryer or large heavy-based saucepan, heat the oil to 180°C (350°F), or until a cube of bread dropped into the oil turns golden brown in 15 seconds. Lightly flour the sardines and deep-fry them. When they are golden brown, remove them with a slotted spoon and drain on paper towels. Place a single layer of sardines in a large bowl, cover with a layer of onion, and repeat until all have been layered. Pour over the vinegar from the pan while it's still hot (it should cover the sardines). Cover with plastic wrap and leave for at least 24 hours in the refrigerator before eating.

VARIATION

Replace the sardines with other fish such as small sole (*sfogi*).

NOTE

In winter you can increase the energy value of the marinade by adding a few currants, rehydrated in water beforehand, some pine nuts and a few pinches of ground cinnamon sprinkled over the sardines before pouring over the vinegar cooking liquid.

CALAMARI ALLA GRIGLIA

GRILLED SQUID

This mollusc is very common in the Adriatic. There are different sizes and they are fished throughout the year. Up to 5 cm (2 inches) long, they are called calamaretto *(small squid). These are very tender and eaten whole without cleaning them, deep-fried or stewed. Over 20 cm (8 inches), they are tougher and eaten stuffed.*

SERVES 6 PREPARATION TIME: 30 MINUTES COOKING TIME: 10 MINUTES

30 small squid (about 10 cm/4 inches long)
A little olive oil
1 teaspoon chopped flat-leaf (Italian) parsley

To clean the squid: Using your fingers, pull out the insides, remove the backbone, the beak in the middle of the tentacles and the eyes. Remove the skin. Rinse thoroughly with water. Heat a grill pan (or a conventional frying pan) on medium heat and cook the whole squid with their tentacles until they are golden brown (allow 3 minutes per side). Season with salt and pepper. Serve with a drizzle of olive oil and sprinkled with parsley.

VARIATION

For deep-fried squid: In a deep-fryer or large heavy-based saucepan, heat 1 litre (35 fl oz/4 cups) of oil to 180°C (350°F), or until a cube of bread dropped into the oil turns golden brown in 15 seconds. Cut the squid into rings, dip them in flour, then deep-fry them until golden brown. Drain on paper towels and serve hot.

ACCIUGHE MARINATE

MARINATED ANCHOVIES

This antipasto is a great classic of Venetian cuisine. I enjoyed it at the restaurant Antiche Carampane. The most important thing is the freshness of the anchovies, the quality of the vinegar and olive oil and the flavour of the accompanying bread.

SERVES 6 PREPARATION TIME: 30 MINUTES
MARINATING TIME: 1 HOUR RESTING TIME: 30 MINUTES

500 g (1 lb 2 oz) very fresh anchovies
1 white onion, thinly sliced
185 ml (6 fl oz/¾ cup) good-quality white wine vinegar
2–3 tablespoons olive oil
2 tablespoons chopped flat-leaf (Italian) parsley
1 handful of capers, rinsed
1 handful of pomegranate seeds

Clean the anchovies by breaking the backbone just behind the head and pulling so the insides come out with the head. Slice open the belly, remove any remaining insides and cut off the tail. Rinse and dry with paper towels. Place the anchovies in a deep dish with the onion, season with salt and pepper and pour over the white wine vinegar. Let them marinate for 1 hour in the refrigerator, covered with plastic wrap. Drain, then arrange on a plate, drizzle with the olive oil and scatter the parsley and capers. Garnish with the pomegranate seeds. Wait 30 minutes before serving.

VARIATION

The vinegar can be replaced with the same quantity of lemon juice.

POLENTA & SCHIE

POLENTA & LAGOON PRAWNS

Schie (pronounced 'ski-eh') are tiny live prawns, which are even more delicious if you have the patience to shell them! Otherwise, pan-fry them in a little oil and eat them whole.

SERVES 6 PREPARATION TIME: 30 MINUTES
COOKING TIME: 10 MINUTES TO 1 HOUR

1 kg (2 lb 4 oz) small raw prawns (shrimp)
1 tablespoon olive oil
1 tablespoon chopped flat-leaf (Italian) parsley
Salt and pepper

THE POLENTA
1 litre (35 fl oz/4 cups) water
1½ teaspoons coarse salt
250 g (9 oz) polenta (cornmeal) (see note below)

To make the polenta: Bring the water to the boil, add the salt, then add the polenta in a stream and whisk for 2–3 minutes to prevent lumps from forming (follow the instructions on the packet). Stir frequently. The polenta should be quite liquid, if not, gradually add more boiling water. Cook for about 1 hour (or according to packet instructions if you are using a quick-cooking polenta).

Steam the prawns until they turn pink. Peel the prawns (or they can also be eaten unpeeled) and dress them with the olive oil and parsley. Season with salt and pepper. Place some wet polenta on plates and top with a few prawns. Serve hot.

VARIATION

You can also deep-fry the prawns in a little oil without peeling them, drain them on paper towels and season with salt before serving.

NOTE

If you have time, use white slow-cooking polenta, brought back from Venice.

SESTRIERE — SAN POLO

The Rialto Market: Not to be missed under any circumstances! Go in the morning before 7 am to witness the spectacle of the boats unloading their goods. The Rialto Market is open from 7 am to 1 pm except Sundays and Mondays. It is a unique spot looking over the Grand Canal: on one side are two ancient open market halls housing the *pescheria* (the fishmongers), and on the other side is the open-air fruit and vegetable market. For fish, visit the stall of **Marco Bergamasco (1)** in the main aisle of the market. He supplies the best restaurants in Venice. This fishmonger specialises in fish from the Adriatic. First come first served! Opposite the fish market is the **Pronto Pesce (2)** seafood delicatessen. This is a delicatessen-style eatery where you can eat in or take away traditional or inventive dishes according to the chef's whim. On Saturday mornings, you can often enjoy raw fish and oysters there. Next door on the right, in the Campo Beccarie on the corner with the Ruga del Spezier, stop in at Pietro's **Bar Fiamma (3)** for a coffee, an *orzo* or a *pallina* (100 ml/3½ fl oz) of wine. You can hear the stallholders from the market talk to each other in the Venetian dialect in this little bar. If you ever happen to ask them for information, they will immediately fill you in ... on everything!

From Campo Beccarie, leaving the fish market, take the tiny *calle* that leads off straight ahead. Turn left into the Calle ai do Mori. Immediately on your left you will find *il bàcaro* **I Do Mori (4)**. The counter is always full of *cicheti*! I Do Mori is open non-stop from early morning until early evening. On your right you will find my favourite bàcaro: **All'Arco (5)**, open from 8 am to 3 pm. Have a Venetian-style breakfast here with specialities from the lagoon. I love its family atmosphere. Try the different *baccalà* and the sardines *in saor* made by Signora Mary, the mother of Mr Pinto, the owner, who serves his spritz with a smile. Signora Mary has taught her grandson Matteo the secrets of her traditional recipes. In addition to these, Matteo invents new *cicheti* every day using the finest cured meats, cheeses and vegetables from the lagoon. Outside tables are rare and seized immediately, but the *cicheti* are just as delicious eaten standing up. Not far away in the Calle do Spade is the **Cantina Do Spade (6)** with its comfortable inside tables, rare enough to deserve special mention. Cantina Do Spade has a *cicheti* counter and offers a small menu, not to mention the risotto served at 1 pm. If you would like to eat in a lovely little restaurant serving traditional and refined Venetian cooking, book a table at **Antiche Carampane (7)**. It's hidden away, far from the crowds. Take Calle dei Botteri and turn right into Rio Terà delle Carampane. You will be enchanted by the charm of the place, a few quiet tables outside and family hospitality. Try the *spaghetti cassiopipa*.

Not far from the Rialto is the Cà Pesaro Museum, a magnificent palace overlooking the Grand Canal. This is a modern art museum that has a large collection of oriental art as well as the famous Salomé (*Judith II*) by Klimt. Have a seat in the cafeteria which has a view of the Grand Canal! Admire the beautiful San Giacomo dell'Orio church nearby.

FOR FOOD SHOPPING

After the fish and vegetable market, head to the Campo Bella Vienna where you will find the **Casa del Parmigiano (8)** for all the local specialities: cheeses, cured meats and other fine food items (see the gourmet shopping notes on pages 260–4). Sample the fresh cheeses that don't travel well on the spot, such as *casatella*, a soft creamy cheese that looks like *stracchino*, the very creamy local ricotta and the fresh mascarpone sold in bulk (except in summer). All the gourmet food stores are here. Just next door, on the same Campo Bella Vienna, is the tiny wine-bar **Al Marcà (9)**. It offers a wide and delicious variety of *piccoli panini* and an excellent local wine, ideal for a quick snack. You will not find anywhere to sit down, but space to chat in the open air, which is rare in Venice. A glass in one hand, a *panino* in the other, it's a Venetian meeting place. Continue your Ruga del Spezier shopping at **Mascari (10)** for its spices and dried fruits, condiments and biscuits. Close by, take a look at the **Laguna Carni (11)** butcher shop, with its tripe, *musetti* and *castrà* (mutton), which are used to make traditional dishes.

Coffee break. In Ruga Vecchia San Giovanni, take the Calle dei Cinque and have your coffee at the **Caffè del Doge (12)** (7 am to 7 pm), which offers a wide selection of quality coffees. Try the *Doge rosso* or *Doge nero*. The Caffè del Doge also has a wide selection of fresh fruit juices. Next door, in the same Ruga Vecchia San Giovanni, is **Aliani (13)**, with its 1970s décor and a deli counter. Try the sardines *in saor* and the *baccalà* prepared in multiple ways. Head down Ruga Vecchia San Giovanni and stop in Campiello dei Meloni at **Rizzardini (14)**. Linger under the spell of this old *pasticceria* where you can enjoy your order at the counter: *caffè*, *orzo macchiato* or *cioccolata calda* served with Venetian biscuits or *una pastina*.

Lunch break. Between the Campo Bella Vienna and the Campo San Giacomo at the foot of the Rialto Bridge, walk through the so-called Banco Giro walkway. Among the old shops of the Erbaria market you will find *bàcari* such as the **Osteria Bancogiro (15)** with its large terrace overlooking the Grand Canal. Everything here is original and good: eggplant-lardo-octopus tramezzini, home-made *bigoli in salsa* served with a cardoon purée. There are tables inside.

PRIMI PIATTI

PASTA, RAVIOLI, GNOCCHI, RISOTTO AND SOUP

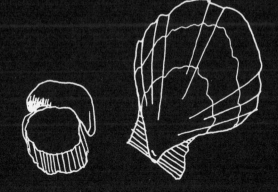

PASTA FATTA IN CASA

FRESH HOME-MADE PASTA

<u>SERVES</u> 6 <u>PREPARATION TIME:</u> 40 MINUTES
<u>RESTING TIME:</u> 30 MINUTES TO 2 HOURS

600 g (1 lb 5 oz/4 cups) '00' strong flour
6 eggs, at room temperature

WHOLEMEAL PASTA
600 g (1 lb 5 oz/4 cups) wholemeal (whole-wheat) flour (or an
    equal mixture of wholemeal and buckwheat flour)
6 eggs, at room temperature

Place the flour on your work surface, make a well in it and break in the eggs. Beat
the eggs with a fork. Use your fingertips to incorporate the flour then work the
dough with the palm of your hand for 5–10 minutes. Add a little flour if the dough is
sticky. When it becomes smooth, form into a ball, wrap in plastic wrap and let it rest
at room temperature for 30 minutes to 2 hours: this will make it easier to roll out.

ROLLING OUT THE PASTA DOUGH

Using 60 g (2¼ oz) portions of dough, roll out either by hand or using a machine.

By hand: Flour your work surface frequently and roll out the dough with a rolling pin,
always starting from the middle. You have to work fairly quickly, otherwise the dough
can dry out. The thickness may not be even.

By machine: Flatten the dough with the palm of your hand. Flour it lightly and feed
it through the machine, with the rollers opened to the widest setting. Fold the dough
in three and feed it back through the machine. Repeat the process until you have a
fairly regular rectangle. Now fold the dough in half and feed it through the machine
several times, gradually narrowing the rollers.

<u>TIPS</u>

Always work with small portions of dough and keep the remaining dough wrapped or
in a plastic bag so it doesn't dry out. Flour the work surface frequently but remove
excess.

For a firmer pasta, replace a third of the flour with fine durum wheat semolina.

CUTTING THE PASTA

Dry out the pasta sheets a little (10 minutes) on a cloth sprinkled with flour so they
don't stick. In Veneto, a special extruder is used for cutting bigoli–wholemeal long
tubular pasta. Otherwise, use a pasta machine.

If cutting by hand, roll the pasta sheets loosely, use a sharp knife and cut the sheets
of pasta into sections, about 5 mm (¼ inch) wide for tagliolini, 1 cm (½ inch) for
tagliatelle, 1.5 cm (⅝ inch) for pappardelle. Unroll the pasta and arrange them in
nests on a cloth. Keep them away from moisture and cook within 2 days. To make
lasagne, cut 40 x 12 cm (16 x 4½ inch) strips that can be cut again depending on the
dish used.

COOKING THE PASTA

Bring a large saucepan of water to the boil. Add salt, then the pasta and let it simmer.
Allow 2–3 minutes cooking time for fresh pasta, 3–4 minutes for dried egg pasta and
10 minutes for dried pasta. The pasta should be *al dente*, taste it before draining.

BIGOLI IN SALSA

BIGOLI WITH ANCHOVY SAUCE

This is a recipe from the Jewish tradition that has become a typical Venetian dish. I love the simplicity and richness of this pasta dish. The anchovies and onions are cooked with a little olive oil until they turn into a sort of cream that dresses the bigoli.

SERVES 6 PREPARATION TIME: 30 MINUTES COOKING TIME: 40 MINUTES

600 g (1 lb 5 oz) bigoli* or wholemeal spaghetti (see page 90)
80 g (2¾ oz) anchovy fillets (preferably in brine)
125 ml (4 fl oz/½ cup) olive oil
1 garlic clove, halved
800 g (1 lb 12 oz) onions, chopped
1 tablespoon chopped flat-leaf (Italian) parsley

Briefly rinse the anchovies under water, and if necessary, clean them, remove their backbone and chop. Heat the oil in a saucepan, melt the anchovies in it, then add the garlic and onion. Gently sauté the onion until translucent, add a few tablespoons of water, cover and cook on low heat until the onion has cooked down (allow 40 minutes). Remove the garlic. Cook the pasta until *al dente* in a large saucepan of boiling salted water. Drain and dress it with the sauce. Serve sprinkled with the parsley.

VARIATIONS

Replace the water in the sauce with white wine or white wine vinegar, add a few chopped salted capers or spices such as cinnamon.

Here is a variation of the recipe that I enjoyed at Bancogiro restaurant in the Rialto: the bigoli are made from buckwheat flour and a cardoon purée is added to the anchovy-onion cream (only 400 g/14 oz of onions are used in this case). Peel 400 g (14 oz) cardoons or globe artichokes, cut into 8 cm (3¼ inch) pieces and boil for 30 minutes in salted water with a tablespoon of flour and the juice of a lemon added so the cardoons don't discolour. Purée two-thirds of the cardoons and add them to the anchovy-onion sauce. Sauté the remaining cardoons in olive oil and add them to the sauce as well.

* Bigoli, a typical Veneto pasta, is shaped like thick spaghetti, originally made from soft wheat flour, water and salt. Today there are several variations: using wholemeal (wholewheat) flour, and/or buckwheat flour mixed with white flour, with eggs ...

PASTA CON LE VONGOLE

PASTA WITH CLAMS

Vongole are very common in the Adriatic and are harvested throughout the year. The name of these molluscs is caparossoli in Venetian (vongole veraci in Italian). They are the most prized species of clam. They have concentric and radial grooves and two siphons that come out of the shell. You will find the signature flavour of Venice in this recipe. The vongole are flavoured with garlic, parsley and olive oil. There's no tomato sauce! And remember that with seafood you don't add parmesan!

SERVES 6 PREPARATION TIME: 30 MINUTES COOKING TIME: 20 MINUTES
SOAKING TIME: 2 TO 4 HOURS

500 g (1 lb 2 oz) spaghetti or bigoli (see page 90)
1 kg (2 lb 4 oz) *vongole veraci (caparossoli or other grooved clams)*
Coarse salt
80 ml (2½ fl oz/⅓ cup) olive oil
3 garlic cloves, halved
125 ml (4 fl oz/½ cup) white wine
½ a bunch of flat-leaf (Italian) parsley, chopped
Chopped chilli (optional)

Wash the clams thoroughly under running water. Soak them for 2–4 hours in water with the coarse salt so they disgorge their sand. Discard any clams that are already open. Heat 1 tablespoon of the oil in a deep frying pan on high heat with 2 half cloves of garlic. Add the clams and wine and cover the pan. After 2 minutes, shake the pan frequently so the heat is well distributed. As soon as the clams open, stir in half the parsley and pour them into a colander, reserving the juices. Discard any clams that haven't opened. Strain the cooking juices through a very fine sieve (or a lightweight fabric) to remove any residual sand and set aside. Shell half the clams and keep warm.

Bring a large saucepan of water to the boil, add salt and cook the spaghetti until almost *al dente*. Meanwhile, rinse out the frying pan and heat the remaining garlic in the remaining oil. Add the cooking juices from the clams and bring to the boil. Add the spaghetti to the pan and finish cooking the pasta in the clam juices, stirring on high heat. A minute before serving, add the shelled and unshelled clams. Remove the garlic. Serve hot with freshly ground pepper, the rest of the parsley and a little chopped chilli, if you like.

TIPS

It's important not to overcook molluscs, or they become rubbery.
Don't add salt because the liquid from the clams is already salty.

SPAGHETTONI ALLA BUSARA

SPAGHETTONI WITH SCAMPI

Venice is famous for its scampi, with its tender meat and subtle flavour thanks to the shallow waters of the Adriatic Sea. Seafood tastes better here. This delicious recipe comes to us from the Istrian coast between Slovenia and Croatia, formerly a Venetian 'factory' or trading post. The best season for scampi is spring, when the head of the female is full of coral.

SERVES 6 PREPARATION TIME: 45 MINUTES COOKING TIME: 30 MINUTES

1 kg (2 lb 4 oz) whole scampi (langoustines, red-claw crayfish or large prawns/shrimp)
1 large onion, finely chopped
1-2 small dried chillies
3 tablespoons olive oil, plus extra for drizzling
2 garlic cloves
185 ml (6 fl oz/¾ cup) dry white wine
1 tablespoon chopped flat-leaf (Italian) parsley
2 tablespoons home-made breadcrumbs
2 kg (4 lb 8 oz) tomatoes, peeled, seeded and diced (see note below)
600 g (1 lb 5 oz) spaghettoni (thick spaghetti)

Wash the scampi well. Using a pair of scissors, make an incision in the back and remove the black intestine using a toothpick. Don't shell them. Sauté the onion and chilli in a frying pan with the oil and garlic for 2 minutes on medium heat. Add the scampi, sauté on high heat for a few moments before adding the white wine. Boil the liquid on a high boil for 30 seconds. Turn over the scampi, season them with salt and sprinkle with half the parsley and the breadcrumbs. Remove the scampi and set aside. Add the tomato to the pan and cook for 10 minutes on low heat. Return the scampi to the pan and cook for another 5 minutes. Remove the garlic.

Bring a large saucepan of water to the boil, add salt, then the pasta. Stir well. Cook the pasta until *al dente*, drain and mix with the sauce for 1-2 minutes on the heat. Serve with a drizzle of olive oil and sprinkle with the remaining parsley.

NOTE

To peel tomatoes: Make an incision in the base of the tomatoes, and drop them in boiling water for 2 minutes, then refresh in cold water. Remove skin.

To seed: Cut the tomato in half and scoop out the seeds with a teaspoon.

TAGLIOLINI NERI ALLE MAZZANCOLLE

BLACK TAGLIOLINI WITH PRAWNS, ASPARAGUS & PEAS

For this springtime dish, I suggest you make the black tagliolini yourself. Buy raw prawns: mazzancolle (caramote prawns) from Venice are very tasty. You can also use scampi. Choose seasonal vegetables and cook them quickly so they stay crisp. Lift the whole dish with lemon zest and fresh herbs. A delight!

SERVES 6 PREPARATION TIME: 30 MINUTES FOR THE PASTA
+ 45 MINUTES COOKING TIME: 30 MINUTES

HOME-MADE TAGLIOLINI
500 g (1 lb 2 oz/3⅓ cups) plain (all-purpose) flour
4 eggs
1 egg yolk
8 g (¼ oz) cuttlefish or squid ink (available from the fishmonger)

THE SAUCE
250 g (9 oz) fresh shelled peas
12 green asparagus spears, tips separated
80 ml (2½ fl oz/⅓ cup) olive oil
24 raw prawns (shrimp), or *mazzancolle* tails (see above)
Grated zest of 1 organic lemon
1 tablespoon chopped flat-leaf (Italian) parsley or basil
Freshly ground black pepper

Make the home-made pasta as explained on page 90, adding the cuttlefish ink with the eggs. Add a little more flour to the dough if needed. Cut the pasta in a pasta maker if you have one. Otherwise, wait for 10 minutes so the pasta dries out a little before rolling it up and cutting into 5 mm (¼ inch) wide strips.

Cook the peas for a few minutes (depending on their size) in a little boiling salted water. Repeat the process with the asparagus tips. Refresh under cold water. Discard the bottom 2 cm (¾ inch) of the asparagus spears, slice the remainder into rounds and sauté in a little of the olive oil for a few minutes on medium heat: they should stay crisp. Season with salt and freshly ground pepper. Peel the prawns and quickly brown them in a pan with a little olive oil on medium-high heat. Season them with salt then add the lemon zest, peas and asparagus.

Cook the pasta until *al dente* in a large saucepan of salted water and drain, reserving 2 ladlefuls of the cooking water. Return the pasta to the heat with the vegetables and prawns, 2 tablespoons of olive oil, the parsley and the reserved pasta water. Stir to coat the pasta, until the water is almost absorbed. Serve immediately.

BIGOLI IN CASSOPIPA

BIGOLI WITH SEAFOOD & SWEET SPICES

*This is a recipe flavoured with sweet spices, as was common
practice when the Republic of Venice, at its peak, dominated
maritime trade. You will still find this dish on the menu at the
restaurant Antiche Carampane. Here is their delicious recipe.*

SERVES 6 PREPARATION TIME: 1 HOUR COOKING TIME: 45 MINUTES
SOAKING TIME: 3 HOURS

500 g (1 lb 2 oz) spaghetti or bigoli (see page 90)
3 kg (6 lb 12 oz) molluscs and shellfish (mussels, clams, cockles, razor clams ...)
Coarse salt
800 g (1 lb 12 oz) squid, cleaned*
Olive oil
3 garlic cloves
1 onion, finely chopped
1 carrot, finely chopped
1 celery stalk, finely chopped
170 ml (5½ fl oz/⅔ cup) white wine
1 clove
1 pinch of ground cinnamon
1 pinch of freshly grated nutmeg
1 bay leaf
1 thyme sprig
125 ml (4 fl oz/½ cup) tomato passata (puréed tomatoes)
1 tablespoon chopped flat-leaf (Italian) parsley

Scrub the mussels, pulling out their hairy beards, and carefully clean the other shellfish.
Soak them all for at least 3 hours in water with some coarse salt so they disgorge their
sand. Cut the squid into small pieces. In a large saucepan, sauté each shellfish separately,
with a little olive oil and a clove of garlic for each, until the shells open. Discard any that
do not open. Strain and reserve the cooking juices, removing any traces of sand. s

In a flameproof pot, preferably an earthenware one, sauté the onion, carrot and celery in a
little olive oil on medium heat. Add the squid and pan-fry for 2 minutes, then add the white
wine. After 2 minutes, add a little of the strained shellfish juices, the spices, bay leaf and
thyme. Lower the heat and simmer, adding the strained juices as needed: the sauce should
be syrupy. Add the shellfish and simmer for another 2 minutes.

Cook the pasta until *al dente*. Drain the pasta and dress with the *cassopipa* sauce,
1 tablespoon of warmed tomato passata per person, a drizzle of olive oil and parsley.

NOTE

This dish comes from Chioggia, a small fishing port at the entrance to the lagoon. Its
name, *bigoli in cassopipa*, comes from the verb *pipare* which here means 'to simmer'. Once
upon a time the leftovers from the market were simmered in an earthenware pot in a
corner of a wood-fired stove. Today, this recipe has become a classic Venetian dish.

* See page 80 for how to prepare squid.

Antiche
Carampane

RIGATONI AL BACCALÀ E CIPOLLA

RIGATONI WITH DRIED COD & ONIONS

This recipe is inspired by a dish I tasted at the restaurant Al Covo.
It's another way to enjoy baccalà, Venice's signature ingredient.
There's also cinnamon and pistachio in this recipe, reminding us of
the Venice of old which traded spices and nuts with the East.

SERVES 6 PREPARATION TIME: 30 MINUTES COOKING TIME: 30 MINUTES

600 g (1 lb 5 oz) rehydrated or desalted cod*
1 garlic clove
1 bay leaf or 1 flat-leaf (Italian) parsley sprig
1 large handful of raw pistachio kernels
3 onions, thinly sliced
2 tablespoons olive oil
2-3 pinches of ground cinnamon
500 g (1 lb 2 oz) rigatoni
A few leaves of fresh marjoram, or flat-leaf (Italian) parsley, chopped

Place the cod in a saucepan with the garlic and bay leaf, cover with cold water, bring
to the boil and simmer for 5 minutes. Cool the cod in the water then remove (don't
throw the water out!), and coarsely flake the cod between your fingers, making sure
to remove any bones. Toast the pistachios in a dry frying pan for 3-4 minutes, or
until starting to colour. When they have cooled, chop them roughly and set aside.
Gently sauté the onion in a frying pan in the oil until it is translucent. Sprinkle
with cinnamon, season with salt, add the cod and simmer for 5 minutes, adding
a little of the cod cooking liquid. Check the level of salt and season with pepper.

Cook the pasta until almost *al dente* in a large quantity of boiling salted water,
drain and finish cooking the pasta in the cod-onion sauce, thinned out with some
of the cod poaching water. Stir on the heat until the pasta is cooked and well
coated with sauce. Add the marjoram or parsley and the pistachios. Serve hot.

RECOMMENDATION

For this recipe, replace the dried cod from Venice, with some flaked salt cod,
which doesn't take long to desalt (allow 30 minutes under running water), or see
instructions on page 11.

* See page 11 for how to prepare dried or salted cod.

PAPPARDELLE AI FEGATINI

PAPPARDELLE WITH CHICKEN LIVERS

*This is a practical and very tasty recipe. The pasta is
cooked in stock and dressed with sautéed chicken livers and
parmesan. The tradition is to serve the pasta with a little
chicken stock … with home-made stock it's even better!*

SERVES 6 PREPARATION TIME: 20 MINUTES COOKING TIME: 20 MINUTES

HOME-MADE PAPPARDELLE
400 g (14 oz/2⅔ cups) strong flour
8 egg yolks

THE SAUCE
400 g (14 oz) chicken livers (see recommendation below)
A few sage leaves
50 g (1¾ oz) butter
1 tablespoon olive oil
2 litres (70 fl oz/8 cups) home-made chicken stock, or made with an organic stock cube
50 g (1¾ oz) parmesan cheese, grated

Make the pasta as explained on page 90 or use ready-made.

To make the sauce: Clean the chicken livers. Remove any fatty parts, wash the
livers and dry them with paper towels. Dice. Brown the liver with the sage for
5 minutes in a large frying pan with half the butter and the olive oil on medium-
high heat, season with salt and pepper. Bring the stock to the boil in a saucepan
and add the pasta. Once the pasta is *al dente*, drain it, and add it to the livers,
with a ladleful of the cooking stock. Stir on high heat, reduce the liquid a little,
add the remaining butter in pieces and the grated parmesan. Serve immediately.

RECOMMENDATION

Make sure the livers are very fresh and don't have any greenish (gall) spots. Buy
livers that are pink, as they're more delicate and flavoursome than the bright red
ones. Preferably soak the livers for 30 minutes in water to remove the blood.

NOTE

Poultry livers and giblets are very common in Venetian cuisine. The famous
Treviso gastronome Giuseppe Maffioli claims the best-tasting liver is rabbit
liver, then, in order of preference, turkey, duck, goose and chicken.

LASAGNA ALLE VERDURE DEL MERCATO

LASAGNE WITH MARKET VEGETABLES

A lasagne inspired by the one at the restaurant La Zucca, which I have reworked in my own way using spring vegetables. Instead of béchamel sauce, I suggest ricotta enriched with parmesan … simply de-li-zio-sa!

SERVES 6 PREPARATION TIME: 1 HOUR COOKING TIME: 40 MINUTES

8-10 lasagne sheets (ready-made, or home-made, see page 90)
20 g (¾ oz) butter, plus extra for greasing

THE SAUCE
300 g (10½ oz) shelled peas
12 green asparagus spears, tips separated
2-3 zucchini (courgettes), diced
Olive oil
1 garlic clove, crushed

THE CREAM
500 g (1 lb 2 oz) ricotta cheese
100 ml (3½ fl oz) thin (pouring) cream
100 g (3½ oz) parmesan cheese, grated

To make the sauce: Preheat the oven to 180-200ºC (350-400ºF/Gas 4-6). Cook the peas in boiling salted water for about 10 minutes: they should still be crisp. Blanch the asparagus tips in boiling water for 2 minutes. Discard the tough end of the asparagus spears and cut the rest of the spears into rounds. Cook the asparagus rounds and zucchini separately in a frying pan with a little olive oil and garlic on medium heat for a few minutes: they should be *al dente*. Season with salt.

To make the cream: Combine the ricotta with the cream and two-thirds of the parmesan, season with salt and pepper if necessary. Precook the sheets of lasagne by dropping them into boiling salted water for 2-3 minutes, no more than 4 sheets at a time, otherwise they might stick together. Stop the cooking process by dropping the pasta sheets in a basin of cold water, drain and place on a clean cloth.

Butter a baking dish, make three or four layers of alternating sheets of pasta, cream and vegetables. Finish with a layer of pasta, some ricotta, lots of parmesan and a few dots of butter. Bake for about 20 minutes.

VARIATION

In winter, you can replace these vegetables with leeks, pumpkin, broccoli …

LA·ZUCCA

PASTICCIO DI CRESPELLE AI FUNGHI

CREPE LASAGNE WITH MUSHROOMS

My mamma always makes her lasagne with crespelle: a savoury crepe batter. Restaurants in Veneto often serve crespelle with seasonal vegetables. They are more delicate than lasagne sheets, easy to cut and hold up well to cooking!

SERVES 8 PREPARATION TIME: 1 HOUR COOKING TIME: 1 HOUR
RESTING TIME: 1 HOUR

THE CREPE BATTER
120 g (4¼ oz) plain (all-purpose) flour
3 eggs
20 g (¾ oz) butter, melted, plus extra for cooking
250 ml (9 fl oz/1 cup) milk

THE FILLING
1 kg (2 lb 4 oz) mixed mushrooms
2 tablespoons olive oil
1 garlic clove, halved
1 rosemary stalk, halved
80 g (2¾ oz) parmesan cheese, grated
20 g (¾ oz) butter

THE BÉCHAMEL SAUCE
40 g (1½ oz) butter
40 g (1½ oz) plain (all-purpose) flour
580 ml (20¼ fl oz/2⅓ cups) milk
Freshly grated nutmeg

To make the crepe batter: Place the flour in a mixing bowl and make a well in the centre. Add the eggs, a pinch of salt and the melted butter. Mix to combine. Add the milk to the batter, whisking to prevent lumps. Cover and let the batter rest for 1 hour.

Preheat the oven to 200°C (400°F/Gas 6). For the béchamel sauce, melt the butter in a saucepan and sprinkle in the flour, stirring to combine. When the mixture starts to colour, add the milk, stirring constantly to prevent lumps and cook for 10 minutes on low heat. Season with salt and nutmeg and allow to cool. For the filling, clean the mushrooms and cut the largest ones into smaller pieces. Heat the oil in a frying pan with the garlic and rosemary (which will be removed afterwards). Cook each kind of mushroom separately on high heat and let their liquid evaporate. Season with salt. Combine all the mushrooms in the frying pan and cook for a further 2 minutes. Make the crepes in a buttered non-stick frying pan: they need to be quite thin.

Butter a baking dish that fits the size of the crepes, place 1 crepe in the dish and spread a thin layer of béchamel sauce and a layer of mushrooms on top, then sprinkle with parmesan. Repeat this process until you run out of ingredients. Finish with a few dots of butter. Bake for 15 minutes.

LASAGNA AL RADICCHIO

LASAGNE WITH RADICCHIO TARDIVO

*The ex-tra-or-din-ary radicchio tadivo is to be enjoyed in
all its forms, raw or grilled, and it's exquisite pan-fried for
this lasagne ... a must to bring back from Venice!*

SERVES 6 PREPARATION TIME: 1 HOUR COOKING TIME: 40 MINUTES

8 lasagne sheets (ready-made, or home-made, see page 90)

THE FILLING

500 g (1 lb 2 oz) radicchio tardivo (see page 208), or purple radicchio
2 French shallots
2 tablespoons olive oil
80 ml (2½ fl oz/⅓ cup) red wine
100 g (3½ oz) parmesan cheese, grated
20 g (¾ oz) butter, plus extra for greasing

THE BÉCHAMEL SAUCE

40 g (1½ oz) butter
40 g (1½ oz) plain (all-purpose) flour
580 ml (20¼ fl oz/2⅓ cups) milk
Freshly grated nutmeg

Preheat the oven to 180-200°C (350-400°F/Gas 4-6).

To make the béchamel sauce: Melt the butter in a saucepan and sprinkle in
the flour, stirring to combine. When the mixture starts to colour, add the milk,
stirring constantly to prevent lumps and cook for 10 minutes on low heat. Season
with salt and nutmeg. Cover the surface with plastic wrap and allow to cool.

Cut the radicchio into quarters lengthways, wash and dry them and cut into 2 cm
(¾ inch) pieces. Peel and chop the shallots and sauté gently until translucent in
a frying pan with some oil, then add the radicchio and cook for a few minutes,
stirring. Add the red wine, boil for 30 seconds then reduce heat, season with salt
and cook for another 2 minutes.

Precook the sheets of lasagne by dropping them into boiling salted water for
2-3 minutes, no more than 4 sheets at a time, or they can stick together. Drop the
sheets in a basin of cold water to stop the cooking process, then drain them and lay
on a clean cloth.

Butter a baking dish and make four layers, alternating sheets of pasta, béchamel,
radicchio and parmesan. Finish with a layer of pasta, béchamel sauce, radicchio tips,
a few dots of butter and sprinkled parmesan. Bake for 20 minutes, or until golden.

NOTES

Radicchio tardivo is a winter vegetable. A quality greengrocer may be able
to order it in for you, but it will be a little more expensive than in Italy!

RAVIOLI AI CARCIOFI SALTATI

RAVIOLI WITH SAUTÉED ARTICHOKES

You quickly become addicted to the little artichokes from the island of Sant'Erasmo in the Venetian lagoon, but this dish will also be very good made with small purple artichokes!

SERVES 6 PREPARATION TIME: 50 MINUTES COOKING TIME: 20 MINUTES

THE HOME-MADE PASTA
400 g (14 oz/2⅔ cups) plain (all-purpose) flour
4 eggs

THE FILLING
Juice of ½ a lemon
6-8 small purple artichokes
2 tablespoons olive oil
2 garlic cloves, halved
80 ml (2½ fl oz/⅓ cup) white wine, or water
1 tablespoon chopped flat-leaf (Italian) parsley
100 g (3½ oz) cooked potato, mashed
4 tablespoons grated parmesan cheese

THE SAUCE
40 g (1½ oz) butter, melted
6 sage leaves
1 tablespoon chopped flat-leaf (Italian) parsley
40 g (1½ oz) parmesan cheese, grated

Make the pasta as explained on page 90.

To make the filling: Add lemon juice to some water. Discard the dark green leaves of the artichokes (about a dozen leaves) and drop the trimmed artichokes in the lemon water to prevent them from discolouring. Cut the artichokes into thin segments and sauté in a frying pan in the olive oil and garlic on medium heat for a few minutes. Add the wine or water and cook for a few minutes until tender. Be careful not to burn them! Season with salt. Remove from the heat and sprinkle with the parsley and a little pepper. Chop up a third of the artichokes with a knife and mix them with the mashed potato and the parmesan for the filling. Check the seasoning. Set aside the rest for presentation.

Working with small amounts of pasta dough (about 60 g/2¼ oz), roll out the dough thinly on a floured work surface. Place the filling on the pasta at 5 cm (2 inch) intervals using 2 teaspoons. Cover with a second sheet of pasta. Press around the filling with your fingers to remove any air. Cut triangles using a pastry wheel, seal the edges by pressing them together with your fingers and place the ravioli on a floured cloth. Cook the ravioli in boiling salted water in batches for about 5 minutes (depending on the thickness of the pasta), then remove using a slotted spoon. Dress the ravioli with the melted butter mixed with a little of the pasta cooking water and the sage, add the parsley and sprinkle with parmesan before serving with the reserved artichokes.

RAVIOLI AI GAMBERI

RAVIOLI WITH PRAWNS & CRISP VEGETABLES

This dish works best when the fish is only just cooked and the vegetables are still crisp. Feel free to vary it with any seasonal vegetables …

SERVES 6 PREPARATION TIME: 50 MINUTES COOKING TIME: 10 MINUTES

THE HOME-MADE PASTA
400 g (14 oz/2⅔ cups) plain (all-purpose) flour
4 eggs

THE FILLING
800 g (1 lb 12 oz) cooked fish fillets (sea bass, sea bream
   monkfish, swordfish), finely chopped
150–200 g (5½–7 oz) ricotta cheese
Grated zest of 1 organic lemon
12 basil leaves, chopped
Olive oil

THE SAUCE
2 small zucchini (courgettes), diced
2 celery stalks, diced
Olive oil
1 onion, diced
12 prawns (shrimp), preferably raw, with or without their heads
3 tomatoes, peeled, seeded and diced (see note page 96)
1 handful of basil

Make the pasta as explained on page 90.

To make the filling: Combine the fish with the ricotta, lemon zest, basil, a drizzle of olive oil, salt and pepper. Working with small amounts of pasta dough, about 60 g (2¼ oz), roll out the dough very thinly and cut out 8 cm (3¼ inch) squares. Place a generous teaspoonful of filling in the middle. Fold the pasta into a triangle and seal the edges well by brushing them with a little water and pressing them together with your fingers. Fold two corners of the pasta around your index finger to bring them together. Place the ravioli on a cloth sprinkled with flour or semolina.

To make the sauce: Sauté the zucchini and celery separately in a frying pan in a little oil for a few minutes on medium heat and season with salt: they need to stay crisp. Sweat the onion in the frying pan, add the prawns and sauté them for 2 minutes on medium heat. Add the zucchini, celery, tomato and a few basil leaves and stir over the heat for 1 minute. Cook the ravioli in boiling salted water for 5 minutes. Remove them with a slotted spoon, then gently combine with the sauce on the heat, adding a little of the cooking water, freshly ground black pepper and a dash of olive oil.

GNOCCHI DI PATATE

POTATO GNOCCHI

Potato gnocchi are a speciality of northern Italy, specifically of Veneto. When I was a child, I loved making them with my mother. I remember her saying to me: 'The best gnocchi are home-made gnocchi!' I can confirm this is the case! Gnocchi need to be made just before serving. If you wait too long to eat them, they no longer have the same texture.

SERVES 6 PREPARATION TIME: 50 MINUTES
COOKING TIME: 45 MINUTES

1 kg (2 lb 4 oz) potatoes, for mashing
300 g (10½ oz/2 cups) plain (all-purpose) flour
1 egg
2 pinches of freshly grated nutmeg
3 pinches of salt

Wash the potatoes and steam them for 40 minutes or boil in salted water. Peel and mash the potatoes directly on a floured work surface, then let them cool a little. Flour your hands, make a well in the mashed potato and put three-quarters of the flour, the egg, nutmeg and salt in the middle. Mix from the middle outwards and add more flour if necessary: the mixture should be smooth and pliable. With floured hands, make 1.5 cm (⅝ inch) thick sausages and cut these into 2 cm (¾ inch) pieces. You can roll the pieces on the back of a floured parmesan grater, pressing them with your fingertips to make ridges. Place the gnocchi on a floured cloth.

Bring a large quantity of salted water to the boil and add the gnocchi in two batches. As soon as they rise to the surface, remove them with a slotted spoon. Toss the gnocchi in the sauce of your choice.

RECOMMENDATION

If you don't eat the gnocchi right away, I suggest you precook them, refreshing them under cold water to stop the cooking process. Drain and oil the gnocchi and then you can refrigerate them for 24 hours. To reheat them, you just need to drop them into boiling water again or sauté them in a frying pan in a fairly liquid sauce.

GNOCCHETTI AI CROSTACEI

SMALL GNOCCHI WITH CRUSTACEANS, TOMATOES & HERBS

Gnocchetti is the diminutive form of gnocchi: in Italian you add an ending to the word to mean big or small! Gnocchetti are small gnocchi dressed with canoce (mantis prawns) and flavoured with herbs. At the osteria Alle Testiere, the sauce is flavoured with wild fennel. Alternatively, use 1 level teaspoon of fennel seeds crushed using a pestle and mortar.

SERVES 6 PREPARATION TIME: 1 HOUR COOKING TIME: 15 MINUTES

THE GNOCCHI
1 kg (2 lb 4 oz) potatoes, for mashing
320 g (11¼ oz) plain (all-purpose) flour (approximately)
1 egg + 1 egg yolk
3 pinches of salt

THE SAUCE
1 onion, finely chopped
3 tablespoons olive oil
Grated zest of 1 organic lemon
500 g (1 lb 2 oz) tomatoes, peeled, seeded and diced (see note page 96)
30 raw mantis prawns (shrimp), or other variety of your choosing in their shell
1 tablespoon chopped herbs (flat-leaf (Italian) parsley, dill)
80 ml (2½ fl oz/⅓ cup) dry white wine

Make the gnocchi dough as explained on page 116. With floured hands, roll the dough into 1 cm (½ inch) thick sausages. Cut these sausages into 1 cm (½ inch) sections and place on a floured cloth.

To make the sauce: Sauté the onion in a frying pan in oil on low heat for 5 minutes. Add the lemon zest, tomato, prawns and half the herbs. Season with salt, add the wine and cook on low heat for 4 minutes, covered, without stirring. Let the mixture cool a little. Set aside 12 prawns for presentation. Shell the remaining prawns: Using a pair of scissors, cut the shell along the body and remove the meat, and cut into 2 cm (¾ inch) pieces.

Bring a large quantity of salted water to the boil and add the gnocchi in two batches. As soon as they rise to the surface, remove them with a slotted spoon. Combine them gently with the tomato mixture and prawn pieces for a few moments on low heat (not too long or the crustaceans will become rubbery). Add the remaining herbs and season with pepper. Serve with the reserved prawns.

NOTE
If the sauce is too thin, add a spoonful of breadcrumbs.

VARIATION
Instead of mantis prawns, use uncooked scampi or prawns of choice. Sauté them in a frying pan on high heat for a few minutes with the same ingredients, then shell them.

GNOCCHI AL NERO DI SEPPIA

CUTTLEFISH INK GNOCCHI

These gnocchi, which I enjoyed at the trattoria Altanella in the Giudecca, left a special imprint on my memories of Venice. Chef and owner Stefano revealed his recipe to me, which I have the pleasure of sharing with you!

SERVES 6 PREPARATION TIME: 1 HOUR COOKING TIME: 1 HOUR

THE GNOCCHI
1 kg (2 lb 4 oz) potatoes, for mashing
300 g (10½ oz/2 cups) plain (all-purpose) flour
1 egg
3 cuttlefish or squid ink sacs, or 12 g (½ oz) of cuttlefish
    ink (available from the fishmonger)
3 pinches of salt

THE CUTTLEFISH INK SAUCE
1 kg (2 lb 4 oz) of cuttlefish or squid with their ink sacs or
    8 g (¼ oz) of cuttlefish ink (available from the fishmonger)
Olive oil
2 garlic cloves, halved
1 teaspoon chopped flat-leaf (Italian) parsley
80 ml (2½ fl oz/⅓ cup) white wine
1 tablespoon tomato paste (concentrated purée)
30 g (1 oz) butter

To make the sauce: Clean the cuttlefish by carefully removing their insides and removing their beaks and eyes. Set the ink sacs aside, cut the cuttlefish lengthways and then into small pieces. Heat some olive oil in a saucepan on medium heat and sauté the garlic with the parsley, add the cuttlefish and stir for 2 minutes. Add the white wine, let it boil for 30 seconds, then add the tomato paste and ink and enough water to cover the cuttlefish. Cook on medium heat for 20-40 minutes, uncovered. Taste and remove from heat when the cuttlefish are tender. Remove the garlic and season.

Make the gnocchi as explained on page 116, incorporating the cuttlefish ink into the mashed potatoes at the same time as the egg. With floured hands, roll the dough into 1.5 cm (⅝ inch) thick sausages and cut these into 2 cm (¾ inch) pieces. Place on a floured cloth. Bring a large quantity of salted water to the boil and add the gnocchi in two batches. As soon as they rise to the surface, remove them with a slotted spoon. Combine the gnocchi with the sauce, thinned out with a little of the cooking water. To finish, add the butter, mix well and serve hot.

GNOCCONI COL SUGO D'ANATRA

LARGE GNOCCHI WITH DUCK SAUCE

This recipe is inspired by a dish at the restaurant Al Covo. Gnocconi are large gnocchi eaten with duck sauce and erbe cotte (a mixture of local greens). Duck sauce is a great classic of Veneto cuisine. It also goes well with bigoli (thick hand-made spaghetti), and tagliatelle, with the addition of some tomato sauce.

SERVES 6 PREPARATION TIME: 45 MINUTES COOKING TIME: 1¼ HOURS

FOR THE GNOCCONI
1 quantity gnocchi dough (see page 116)
30 g (1 oz) butter, melted
30 g (1 oz) parmesan cheese, grated

FOR THE DUCK SAUCE
3 duck leg quarters, cut into two pieces
2 tablespoons olive oil
1 carrot, finely chopped
1 celery stalk, finely chopped
1 onion, finely chopped
1 garlic clove, chopped
Bouquet garni (with rosemary and sage)
80 ml (2½ fl oz/⅓ cup) white wine

FOR THE GREENS
500 g (1 lb 2 oz) leafy greens—English spinach, silverbeet (Swiss chard)
   leaves, turnip greens etc.) green part only, cut into strips
1 garlic clove, chopped
1 tablespoon olive oil
Freshly grated nutmeg

Make the gnocchi dough as explained on page 116. With floured hands, roll the dough into 2 cm (¾ inch) thick sausages and cut these into 2-3 cm (¾-1¼ inch) pieces. Place on a floured cloth.

To make the sauce: In a cast-iron pot, brown the pieces of duck in the oil on high heat. Pour off the excess fat. Add the carrot, celery, onion, garlic and the bouquet garni, stir and gently brown for 5 minutes. Next add the wine, boil for 30 seconds, season with salt and cover. Simmer for 1 hour on low heat, adding a little more water if necessary. Remove the bones and skin from the duck, dice the meat and return it to the pot.

Wilt the greens in a frying pan on medium heat with a little olive oil and the garlic. Season with salt and pepper and add 3 pinches of nutmeg. Cook until the water from the greens has evaporated.

Bring a large quantity of salted water to the boil and add the gnocconi in two batches. As soon as they rise to the surface, remove them with a slotted spoon. Dress them with the melted butter and parmesan. Spoon some duck sauce in the bottom of each dish and top with gnocconi and greens.

IL RISOTTO

THE BASIC RECIPE

Risotto rice has been grown on the Po Plain in northern Italy for centuries. Vialone Nano is a typical Veneto variety, ideal for very 'wet' risottos, which is to say all'onda (when you tilt the plate, the risotto slides to the edge forming a wave … un'onda!). Ask for Vialone Nano rice from your Italian grocer. Otherwise, use the Carnaroli variety rather than Arborio, which doesn't hold up as well to cooking.

SERVES 6 PREPARATION TIME: 10 MINUTES COOKING TIME: 30 MINUTES

1.8 litres (63 fl oz) meat or vegetable stock
2 tablespoons olive oil
1 onion, finely chopped
500 g (1 lb 2 oz) rice (preferably Vialone Nano)
2½ tablespoons dry white wine, or stock
30 g (1 oz) cold butter, or 1½ tablespoons olive oil
60 g (2¼ oz) parmesan cheese, grated (half this amount for seafood risottos)

Heat the stock and keep it simmering on the stove. Heat the oil in a heavy-based saucepan on medium heat, add the onion and cook gently for 5 minutes, or until softened. Add the rice and stir for about 2-3 minutes on medium heat with a wooden spoon: it will become translucent. Don't allow it to colour. Add the wine or stock and stir until it is completely evaporated. Season with salt. Add a ladleful of very hot stock and stir as it is absorbed by the rice. Continue to add stock by the ladleful, allowing it to be absorbed by the rice, stirring often. While it cooks, add ingredients depending on the recipe you are using. Season with salt. After cooking for 15-18 minutes, the risotto should be ready. Check the texture and seasoning: the risotto should remain wet and the grains firm. Add a little more stock if needed. Off the heat, incorporate the cold butter in pieces and the parmesan, and stir vigorously for 1 minute (in Italian, this step is called *mantecare*). Cover and let the risotto stand for 2 minutes before serving.

FOR THE STOCK

- vegetable stock: boil 2 litres (70 fl oz/8 cups) of water with 2 onions, 2 carrots, 2 celery stalks, 2 leeks and some salt, cook for 40 minutes to 1 hour, then strain.

- meat stock: add to the basic vegetable stock 500 g (1 lb 2 oz) beef short ribs, a boiling hen, or some chicken thighs and cook for 2 hours. Skim and degrease the stock. Otherwise, use organic or MSG and flavour enhancer-free stock cubes.

- fish stock: sauté 2 sliced onions and 2 sliced leeks in a saucepan in 2 tablespoons olive oil for 5 minutes on medium heat. Add 500 g (1 lb 2 oz) well-cleaned fish trimmings (the fishmonger will give them to you), a bouquet garni and some white peppercorns. Add 2 litres (70 fl oz/8 cups) of cold water, bring to the boil, skim and cook on medium heat for 30 minutes. Adjust the seasoning and strain. Otherwise, use a concentrated fish stock without flavour enhancers.

1000g

RISARE
DE' TACCHI
DAL 1570.

PRODOTTO ITALIANO

RISO
VIALONE
NANO

RISI E BISI

RISOTTO WITH PEAS

This is the traditional dish of the feast day of the city's patron saint, San Marco (Saint Mark), on 25 April, Venice's most important festival. During the time of La Serenissima, the Doge (the elected chief of state) was offered risi e bisi, rice and peas, the first harvest of the lagoon's vegetable gardens. The rice is served very liquid: between a risotto and a minestra, a soup. It can be made like a risotto by gradually adding stock as you cook, which results in a better texture, or by adding all of the stock at once. The proportion of rice is one-third of the unshelled weight of the peas.

SERVES 6 PREPARATION TIME: 15 MINUTES
COOKING TIME: ABOUT 30 MINUTES

1.2 kg (2 lb 10 oz) unshelled peas
1 onion, finely chopped
2 tablespoons olive oil
150 g (5½ oz) pancetta, chopped
400 g (14 oz) rice (preferably Vialone Nano)
1.5 litres (52 fl oz/6 cups) hot chicken or vegetable stock
1 tablespoon chopped flat-leaf (Italian) parsley
Freshly ground black pepper
50 g (1¾ oz) cold butter
60 g (2¼ oz) parmesan cheese, grated

Shell the peas, reserving the pods to flavour the stock. Cook the peas in a very small amount of water, without adding salt, until they are *al dente*, without being overcooked! To make the risotto: Sweat the onion in a saucepan with the olive oil and pancetta. Add the rice and stir for 1-2 minutes on medium heat before adding a ladleful of stock. Let the liquid evaporate and season with salt. Keep adding stock as it is absorbed by the rice, stirring often. After 10 minutes, add the cooked peas. Continue to cook for about 15-18 minutes on medium heat, stirring occasionally. Remove from the heat, add the parsley, pepper, butter and parmesan, and stir vigorously. Let it stand for 2 minutes, covered. Serve *all'onda* (very wet).

VARIATION: RISOTTO PISELLI, VONGOLE & COZZE

Mauro Lorenzon from the Mascareta *enoteca* cooked a fresh pea risotto before my eyes and added cooked and shelled clams and mussels with their exquisite juices … (for the sautéed shellfish recipe, see page 76).

Mauro uses some anchovy *colatura* instead of salt (this is a concentrated anchovy juice, like a Vietnamese fish sauce). He also adds a few spoonfuls of rice flour to the risotto after two ladlefuls of broth, to give creaminess to the risotto without needing butter at the end!

RISOTTO AI FRUTTI DI MARE

SEAFOOD RISOTTO

For this extraordinary risotto, go to the market early and ask for advice on what is best depending on the season and where you are.

SERVES 6 PREPARATION TIME: 1 HOUR SOAKING TIME: 2 HOURS
COOKING TIME: 45 MINUTES

1 litre (35 fl oz/4 cups) hot fish stock (see page 124)
1 tablespoon olive oil
1 onion
400 g (14 oz) rice (preferably Vialone Nano)
185 ml (6 fl oz/¾ cup) dry white wine
1 tablespoon chopped flat-leaf (Italian) parsley
Freshly ground black pepper
70 g (2½ oz) butter
30 g (1 oz) parmesan cheese, grated

THE SEAFOOD
1 kg (2 lb 4 oz) mussels
500 g (1 lb 2 oz) cockles, clams ...
Coarse salt
125 ml (4 fl oz/½ cup) olive oil
2 garlic cloves, halved
½ a bunch of flat-leaf (Italian) parsley, chopped
185 ml (6 fl oz/¾ cup) dry white wine
500 g (1 lb 2 oz) raw prawns (shrimp)
2 fillets red mullet, skin on

Scrub the mussels, pulling out their hairy beards, and carefully clean the other shellfish. Soak them all for 2 hours in water with the coarse salt so they disgorge their sand. Heat 2 tablespoons of oil in a deep frying pan with the garlic and parsley. After a few moments, add the white wine, wait for the liquid to come to the boil, then add the different shellfish separately. As soon as they open, take them out and place them in a bowl. Once all the shellfish are cooked, strain the cooking juices. Reserve about 20 shellfish for presentation. Shell the remainder and set them aside in a little of the strained cooking liquid. Reserve the rest of the juices.

Reserve 6 prawns for presentation. Shell the remainder, crush the shells and add them to the cooking juices (this will flavour the stock for the risotto). Heat 2 tablespoons of oil in a frying pan on high heat. Sauté whole prawns first then set aside and sauté the chopped prawns, season with salt and pepper and set aside. Remove the bones of the red mullet fillets and pan-fry fillets for 2 minutes, skin side down, in 1 tablespoon of olive oil. Season with salt.

Make the risotto according to the basic recipe method (see page 124). Once the wine has evaporated, add the strained shellfish juices and a ladleful of hot stock. Keep adding stock as it is absorbed by the rice, stirring often. Cook for 15–20 minutes. At the end of the cooking time, add the pan-fried prawns, the red mullet fillets and the cooked shelled shellfish and gently combine. Remove from the heat and add the parsley, pepper, butter and parmesan and combine. Let it stand, covered, for 2 minutes. Serve with the whole prawns and unshelled shellfish on top.

RISI E PATATE

POTATO RISOTTO

*A comforting risotto to eat at home when it's cold outside.
Flavoured with a little lardo (preferably lardo di Colonnata),
rosemary and garlic, it becomes irresistible!*

SERVES 6 PREPARATION TIME: 15 MINUTES COOKING TIME: 25 MINUTES

50 g (1¾ oz) lardo or pancetta, 300 g (10½ oz) mashing potatoes,
1 onion, 1 rosemary stalk, 80 ml (2½ fl oz/⅓ cup) olive oil, 350 g (12 oz)
rice (preferably Vialone Nano), 1.5 litres (52 fl oz/6 cups) hot beef
stock, 30 g (1 oz) butter, 60 g (2¼ oz) parmesan cheese, grated

Slice the lardo thinly and sauté it with the diced potato, chopped onion
and rosemary in 2 tablespoons olive oil for 5 minutes. Add the rice and
stir for 2 minutes. Add a ladleful of stock and continue cooking according
to the basic recipe (see page 124). Off the heat, add the butter and
parmesan, stir vigorously, and let it stand for 2 minutes, covered.

RISOTTO ALLA LUGANEGA

RISOTTO WITH SAUSAGE

*In Veneto, there are special sausages for risotto: luganega, made with
spices that make them unique. To be able to bring them back home from
Venice with me, I ask for them to be vacuum-packed. Otherwise, use good
fresh sausages and mix the meat with a little cinnamon and nutmeg!*

SERVES 6 PREPARATION TIME: 20 MINUTES COOKING TIME: 40 MINUTES

2 celery stalks, 80 ml (2½ fl oz/⅓ cup) olive oil, 400 g (14 oz) *luganega* (or good-
quality fresh sausage), 1 onion, 400 g (14 oz) rice (preferably Vialone Nano), 125 ml
(4 fl oz/½ cup) dry white wine, 1.5 litres (52 fl oz/6 cups) hot beef stock, 30 g (1 oz) butter,
60 g (2¼ oz) parmesan cheese, grated

Wash and dice the celery and 60 g (2¼ oz)sauté in 2 tablespoons of oil on
medium heat for 3 minutes, then season with salt. In a non-stick frying pan
without added fat, sauté the sausages without their casings on medium heat
for 3 minutes, then mash the meat with a fork. Pour off the fat. Make the risotto
according to the basic recipe (see page 124). Once the wine has evaporated, add
the sausage meat and celery. Add a ladleful of stock and continue to add as it is
absorbed by the rice, stirring often. Cook for 15–20 minutes. Off the heat, add the
butter and parmesan, stir vigorously and let it stand for 2 minutes, covered.

RISOTTO ALLA ZUCCA

PUMPKIN RISOTTO

SERVES 6 PREPARATION TIME: 20 MINUTES COOKING TIME: 40 MINUTES

1 kg (2 lb 4 oz) pumpkin (winter squash), 2 onions, 2 tablespoons olive oil, 400 g (14 oz) rice (preferably Vialone Nano or Carnaroli), 1.5 litres (52 fl oz/6 cups) chicken stock, 1 pinch of nutmeg, 1 pinch of ground cinnamon, 30 g (1 oz) butter, 60 g (2¼ oz) parmesan cheese, grated

Cut the pumpkin into slices and steam them or cook in a little water. When the pumpkin is *al dente*, after about 10 minutes, remove the skin if it is not an organic pumpkin and dice the flesh. Make the risotto according to the basic recipe (see page 124). After adding a ladleful of broth, add the nutmeg, cinnamon and half the pumpkin. After 10 minutes of cooking, add the rest of the pumpkin (for a firmer texture). Off the heat, add some pepper, the butter and parmesan and stir vigorously. Let the risotto stand for 2 minutes, covered, before serving.

RISOTTO AL NERO DI SEPPIA

CUTTLEFISH INK RISOTTO

SERVES 6 PREPARATION TIME: 45 MINUTES COOKING TIME: 35 MINUTES

600 g (1 lb 5 oz) fresh cuttlefish or squid with their ink sacs (or buy 32 g/1 oz ink from the fishmonger), 3–4 French shallots, 125 ml (4 fl oz/½ cup) olive oil, 1 garlic clove, halved, 250 ml (9 fl oz/1 cup) dry white wine, 400 g (14 oz) rice (preferably Vialone Nano), 1.5 litres (52 fl oz/6 cups) hot fish (or vegetable) stock, 1 tablespoon chopped flat-leaf (Italian) parsley, 30 g (1 oz) cold butter, 30 g (1 oz) parmesan cheese, grated

To prepare the cuttlefish: Separate the head from the body, remove the bone, collect the ink in a small bowl and dilute it in a little stock. Rinse the cuttlefish well, remove the skin and the eyes. Cut into strips. Gently sauté one-third of the finely chopped shallots in a frying pan in 2 tablespoons of oil, add the garlic and cuttlefish and sear on high heat for a few minutes. Add half the wine, let it boil for 30 seconds and season with salt. Set aside. Off the heat, stir the cuttlefish ink into the cooking liquid. Make the risotto according to the basic recipe (see page 124), replacing the onion with the rest of the shallots. Once the wine has evaporated, add the cuttlefish with its juices. Add a ladleful of stock and continue to add more as it is absorbed by the rice, stirring often. Cook for 15–20 minutes. Off the heat, add the parsley, butter and parmesan and mix vigorously. Let it stand for 2 minutes, covered, before serving.

RISOTTO AGLI ASPARAGI BIANCHI

WHITE ASPARAGUS RISOTTO

*May is the time for making the most of the white asparagus. In Veneto,
the varieties from Bassano del Grappa, Badoere and Cimadolmo, near
Treviso, are highly regarded. On the market stalls in the springtime you
also find small wild shoots: bruscandoli (wild hop shoots) or carletti
(Silene vulgaris, or bladder campion), which are very good in a risotto.*

SERVES 6 PREPARATION TIME: 30 MINUTES COOKING TIME: 35 MINUTES

1 kg (2 lb 4 oz) white asparagus spears
1 onion, finely chopped
2 tablespoons olive oil
450 g (1 lb) rice (preferably Vialone Nano)
80 ml (2½ fl oz/⅓ cup) dry white wine
1.5 litres (52 fl oz/6 cups) hot vegetable or meat stock
Freshly ground black pepper
30 g (1 oz) butter
60 g (2¼ oz) parmesan cheese, grated

Wash the asparagus and peel the spears, removing the bottom 3 cm (1¼ inches)
of the spears (the toughest part) but keep to add to the stock. Cut off the
tips and then cut the spears into sections about 1.5 cm (⅝ inch) long.

To make the risotto: Gently sweat the onion in a saucepan in the oil for 5 minutes.
Add the rice. Stir for 2–3 minutes, then add the wine, let it evaporate and
season with salt. Add a ladleful of very hot stock. Add the pieces of asparagus
spear, then more stock as it is absorbed by the rice. After 10 minutes, add the
asparagus tips. The risotto should take 15–20 minutes to cook. Off the heat,
add some pepper, butter and parmesan and stir vigorously. Let it stand for
2 minutes, covered, before serving *all'onda*, which is to say, very 'wet'.

MINESTRONE

Minestrone is a vegetable soup whose ingredients change with the seasons and the cook. There is not a corner of Veneto that doesn't have its own special recipe. The pasta is not essential, but Lamon beans (or dried beans) are almost always included.

SERVES 6 PREPARATION TIME: 30 MINUTES COOKING TIME: 40 MINUTES + 2 HOURS FOR THE DRIED BEANS SOAKING TIME: 12 HOURS

600 g (1 lb 5 oz) fresh beans in their pods, or 200 g (7 oz) dried borlotti or Lamon beans
2 pinches of bicarbonate of soda (baking soda)
2 onions, sliced
2 tablespoons of olive oil, plus extra for drizzling
2 potatoes, diced
2 carrots, diced
2 celery stalks, chopped
2 leeks, pale part only, chopped
½ savoy cabbage, chopped
300 g (10½ oz) butternut pumpkin (winter squash), peeled and diced
6 leaves silverbeet (Swiss chard), green part only, chopped
2 tablespoons chopped flat-leaf (Italian) parsley
50 g (1¾ oz) parmesan cheese, grated (optional)

If you are using dried beans, soak them overnight in a large bowl of water with the bicarbonate of soda. Drain them and simmer for 2 hours in fresh water. Sauté the onion in a large saucepan in the oil on medium heat. Add the potato, carrot, celery, leek, cabbage, pumpkin and silverbeet and the fresh or dried beans and cover with water. Simmer on low heat until the vegetables are tender (20-30 minutes). Once the vegetables are cooked, remove half and purée, then return this purée to the saucepan. Season with salt and pepper. Let the soup rest (the soup is in fact better reheated the next day as the flavours develop). Serve with a drizzle of good-quality olive oil and sprinkle with parsley. A tablespoon of parmesan can be added to each serve.

VARIATION

The vegetables change with the seasons. In summer, you can use green beans, tomatoes, zucchini and basil instead of cabbage, pumpkin and leeks.

ZUPPA DI FAGIOLI E ORZO

BEAN & BARLEY SOUP

This traditional soup is served hot in winter and cold in summer. I always keep a packet of dried borlotti beans in the cupboard, but the best are the ones from Lamon (a village near Feltre in the province of Belluno in Veneto), which are quite floury and have tender skins, perfect for making a thick soup! I recommend bringing some back with you if you go to Veneto.

SERVES 6 PREPARATION TIME: 10 MINUTES
COOKING TIME: AT LEAST 2 HOURS SOAKING TIME: 12 HOURS

300 g (10½ oz) dried Lamon beans or borlotti beans, or
    600 g (1 lb 5 oz) fresh beans in their pods
2 pinches of bicarbonate of soda (baking soda), or a piece of
    kombu seaweed (to make the beans more digestible)
1 onion, finely chopped
1 carrot, finely chopped
1 celery stalk, finely chopped
125 ml (4 fl oz/½ cup) olive oil
30 g (1 oz) lardo, or ham rind
1 rosemary stalk
1 bay leaf
100 g (3½ oz) pearl barley, or pasta

If you are using dried beans, soak them for 12 hours in a large bowl of water with 1 pinch of bicarbonate of soda or half the kombu seaweed, then drain. Sauté the onion, carrot and celery in a saucepan with the olive oil, lardo, rosemary and bay leaf on medium heat. Add the beans, cover with water and add 1 pinch of bicarbonate of soda or the remaining seaweed. Bring to the boil, simmer for about 2 hours, or until the beans are tender, adding boiling water as needed so the beans are always covered. Season with salt at the end of the cooking time. Meanwhile, cook the barley in boiling salted water until tender but still firm to the bite: allow 15 minutes. Purée half the soup in a food processor and return to the saucepan on the heat. When the soup comes to the boil, add the barley and stir for 2 minutes. Serve with a drizzle of good-quality olive oil and one or two turns of the pepper mill.

VARIATION: PASTA E FAGIOLI (BEAN AND PASTA SOUP)

Bean soup served with pasta is more common than bean soup with barley. Short tubular pasta (ditalini) is used, or tagliatelle broken into 10 cm (4 inch) pieces, cooked directly in the soup. Make sure to add water if needed during cooking.

ZUPPA DI PESCE

FISH SOUP

In Venice, you will find all the seafood you need to make a good fish soup at the Rialto Market, a fish market that dates back to the ninth century. If you aren't able (alas!) to get to the Rialto, ask your fishmonger for advice. Every coastal town has its own recipe. Don't forgo the scorpionfish, despite its off-putting appearance. In Italian, scorfano (scorpionfish) is used to mean someone really very ugly! Nevertheless, the scorpionfish gives a lot of flavour to the soup.

SERVES 6 PREPARATION TIME: 1½ HOURS COOKING TIME: 30 MINUTES

1 onion, chopped
1 carrot, chopped
1 celery stalk, chopped
80 ml (2½ fl oz/⅓ cup) olive oil
2.5 kg (5 lb 8 oz) white fish (sea bass, barramundi ...)
125 ml (4 fl oz/½ cup) dry white wine
200 g (7 oz) tomatoes, peeled (see note page 96) and chopped
1 bay leaf
1.5 litres (52 fl oz/6 cups) water
1 garlic clove, halved
600 g (1 lb 5 oz) squid (and/or other molluscs and shellfish)
12 scampi (langoustines, red-claw crayfish), or gamba prawns
   (shrimp), or other large variety of your choosing
A few stalks of flat-leaf (Italian) parsley, chopped
1 loaf country-style bread (sliced and toasted)

Sauté the onion, carrot and celery in 2 tablespoons of the oil in a frying pan on low heat. Meanwhile, wash and clean the fish, gut them, and add the heads, fins and bones to the vegetables in the pan. Sauté everything on medium heat for 2–3 minutes, add the wine, let it evaporate, then add the tomato, bay leaf and water. Simmer gently for 20 minutes then strain the stock. Return to the heat for 2–3 minutes, season with salt and pepper. Cut the fish into pieces. In a heavy-based saucepan, heat the remaining oil with the garlic, add the squid and scampi and cook on high heat for 1 minute, stirring. Add 2 tablespoons of the stock and the pieces of fish. Cook for 5 minutes on low heat, or longer depending on their size. Remove the garlic. If you are using shellfish, cook them separately until they open and add them at the end with their strained juices. Divide the pieces of fish, squid and scampi between some deep plates, pour over the broth, dress with a little olive oil and parsley, season with pepper and serve with toasted bread.

NOTE

In the official version from Chioggia, half a glass of vinegar is used instead of the white wine and there is no tomato. (Tomato has been included in fish soups from the nineteenth century onwards ...)

There's no parmesan cheese in fish soup either!

SOPA COADA

BAKED PIGEON SOUP

This is a soup that is very slowly 'incubated' (covare) in the oven for at least 2 hours. In former times it would have cooked very gently at 70°C (150°F/ Gas ¼) for several hours in the corner of a wood stove. It's a filling dish and eccellente! Serve as a main course, followed or preceded by a salad.

SERVES 6 PREPARATION TIME: 1 HOUR COOKING TIME: 4½ HOURS

1 onion, diced
1 carrot, diced
1 celery stalk, diced
Olive oil
3 pigeons, quartered, or use 1.5 kg (3 lb 5 oz) quail or chicken, including livers
185 ml (6 fl oz/¾ cup) white wine
60 g (2¼ oz) butter
18 slices of good stale bread, crusts removed, or 1 large loaf sandwich bread
100 g (3½ oz) parmesan cheese, grated

THE MEAT STOCK (2 LITRES/70 FL OZ/8 CUPS)
1 carrot
1 onion
1 celery stalk
500 g (1 lb 2 oz) beef short ribs + 1 bone or 2 chicken thighs
The bones of the cooked pigeons

Make the stock the day before if possible. Place carrot, onion (whole but peeled), celery stalk, the beef and bones, well washed, in a large saucepan. Cover with 2.5 litres (87 fl oz/10 cups) water, bring to the boil, season and simmer for 2 hours, skimming regularly.

Preheat the oven to 90°C (190°F/Gas ½). Sauté the onion, carrot and celery in a little oil on medium heat, add the quartered pigeons and brown. Add the wine, let it boil for 30 seconds, add 2 ladlefuls of stock, cover and cook for 30 minutes. Add the pigeon livers 5 minutes before the end of the cooking time. Let the meat cool before cutting it into strips, remove the livers and cut them in half. Add the hot stock and the pigeon bones to the cooking juices from the pigeon. In a buttered baking dish, make a tightly packed layer of slices of buttered bread (the traditional recipe tells you to fry them in butter!), sprinkle with parmesan, top with some pieces of pigeon meat and liver, moisten with a little stock, arrange another layer of bread slices, and so on until all the ingredients are used up (three layers of bread and two layers of pigeon). Add enough stock to cover the bread and bake for 2 hours, basting regularly with stock so the bread stays moist. The *sopa coada* will be better the next day, reheated in the oven. Serve with some extra broth.

SESTRIERE CASTELLO & SAN MARCO

In the Campo dei Santi San Giovanni e Paolo, start with a coffee and a Venetian biscuit or *pastina* (pastry) at **Rosa Salva (1)** *pasticceria*. While you're there, admire the marble counter of the bar where all the *pastine* are on display for you to feast your eyes on or, better still, your mouth! Try the *pastina* with ricotta, rice or semolina custard. If you prefer a savoury start to the day, you can enjoy a *piccolo panino* from **Al Ponte (2)** on the bridge opposite the hospital and the Basilica dei Santi Giovanni e Paolo. In this charming little *bàcaro*, open all day, you will find quality products and good *cicheti*. Alongside Rosa Salva is the **Librairie Française (3)** (French bookstore, Calle Barbaria delle Tole). It's an independent bookstore and a place for cultural debates and exchange. Let them recommend a book or guide to Venice (in French!).

To get back to the lovely Campo Santa Maria Formosa, take the Calle dell'Ospedale to the Calle Lunga Santa Maria Formosa. You will go past the *enoteca* **Mascareta (4)**, but it doesn't open until 7 pm. Come back to this unmissable wine bar for the evening aperitif. It is open until late at night (which is rare in Venice, where the bars tend to close on the early side). It's a mandatory stop for wine aficionados and novices alike. By listening to the good advice and engaging stories of your *Oste* (host), Mauro Lorenzon, you will become an expert yourself. This *enoteca* is known for its *grands crus*, also served by the glass and accompanied by fine products such as wonderful cured meats and cheeses, oysters and a few good little dishes. The place has two beautiful rooms and some old cinema seats outside. A must-visit!

Campo Santa Maria Formosa: a good restaurant in this area is the **Osteria alle Testiere (5)**. From the Campo Santa Maria Formosa take the Calle del Mondo Novo where you'll find the *osteria*. Make sure you book your table in advance, as the restaurant is tiny. Opened by chef Claudio and sommelier Luca, it offers traditional dishes with a creative twist that evokes the era when Venice was engaged in the spice trade. Try the seafood with ginger ... in fact, try the whole menu!

If you take the Salizzada San Lio, you will be heading towards the Rialto. On the opposite side, you're next to a gem. Cross the Campo Santa Maria Formosa, take Ruga Giuffa then Ramo Grimani to discover the fascinating Palazzo Grimani. This hidden palace reopened in late 2008 after extensive restorations that show off the extraordinary decor of the rooms. Admire its courtyard. Not to be missed.

To go to the neighbourhood of the Arsenal and the Corderie that house some of the exhibits of the Venice Biennale, take Fondamenta San Lorenzo, past La Scuola di San Gorgio degli Schiavoni and continue south. It's a very pleasant area, far from the crowds of the Riva degli Schiavoni.

For a gourmet lunch or dinner, visit **Al Covo (6)**, an elegant restaurant in the Campiello della Pescheria. Cesare and Diane, two food enthusiasts, have run this restaurant for over 25 years. They campaign for the promotion of local products like the *pescato*, the fresh local fish. I love the open kitchen when you go in and the two small rooms inside. There are also comfortable outdoor tables. Try their very light *frittura*. Otherwise, ask *il Signor Cesare* for suggestions. There is a large selection of good wines and grappa. If you are looking for more of an 'osteria' feel, try **Corte Sconta (7)** in the Calle del Pestrin. As its name suggests, it's a well hidden spot (*corte sconta* means 'hidden courtyard' in the Venetian dialect)! There's always a lovely atmosphere here. The bonus: a beautiful internal courtyard (rare), a warm welcome and innovative and high-quality Venetian cuisine. The pasta is home-made! Start with the *antipasto misto della casa*, an assortment of fish.

Back on the Riva degli Schiavoni, in one direction are the Giardini (gardens) that host the Biennale in summer, in the other is San Marco. On the Giardini side, you can visit the Museo Storico Navale (naval history museum) to learn everything about the maritime power of *La Serenissima*. You reach the Giardini by Via Garibaldi, a shopping street.

Feel like an ice-cream? **Al Todaro (8)** is the oldest *gelateria* in Venice. In Piazza San Marco, Al Todaro is opposite the *Doge*'s Palace and the San Marco Canal. I remember when I was a child I would have an ice-cream cone before our walk. Sitting down here is an extravagance, better to save your money for Caffè Florian.

A coffee? To fully appreciate the Piazza San Marco, go to one of the most beautiful historic cafés in the world, and the oldest: **Caffè Florian (9)**. It opened in late 1720. Your coffee there will be unforgettable. If it's cold, have *una cioccolata calda con panna* (a hot chocolate with whipped cream).

For an aperitif in an elegant and legendary spot, head for Calle Vallaresso. Next door to the Correr Museum, overlooking the Grand Canal, you will find **Harry's Bar (10)**, opened in 1931 by Giuseppe Cipriani. Hemingway wrote his novel *Across the River and into the Trees* there. This is the birthplace of the *bellini*, the white peach-based cocktail, and the raw beef dish, *carpaccio*. The tradition continues. Sip your white peach bellini while nibbling on a *pierino* (mini croque-monsieur).

SECONDI PIATTI E CONTORNI

FISH, MEAT AND SIDE DISHES

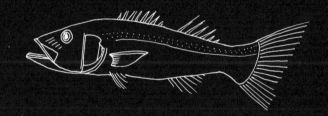

BACCALÀ ALLA VICENTINA

DRIED COD IN SAUCE VICENZA STYLE

This is the Friday meal in Veneto, one of the symbolic dishes of the region made from 'poor' ingredients. It must be served with polenta! In Venice, three good pinches of ground cinnamon are added ... The real recipe is made with dried cod, but if you can't find any, it is also very good with salt cod.

SERVES 6 PREPARATION TIME: 30 MINUTES
COOKING TIME: 2 TO 4 HOURS

1 kg (2 lb 4 oz) rehydrated or desalted cod*
3 anchovy fillets in brine, or 6 anchovy fillets in oil
2 onions, chopped
3 tablespoons olive oil, plus extra for greasing
1 garlic clove, quartered
1 handful of flat-leaf (Italian) parsley leaves, chopped
500 ml (17 fl oz/2 cups) milk
50 g (1¾ oz) parmesan cheese, grated
200 g (7 oz/1⅓ cups) plain (all-purpose) flour

THE POLENTA
2 litres (70 fl oz/8 cups) water
2 teaspoons coarse salt
500 g (1 lb 1 oz/2⅔ cups) polenta (cornmeal)

To make the polenta: Bring the water to the boil, add the salt, then add the polenta in a stream and whisk for 2-3 minutes to prevent lumps from forming (follow the instructions on the packet). Stir frequently. The polenta should be quite liquid, if not, gradually add more boiling water. Cook for about 1 hour (or according to packet instructions if you are using a quick-cooking polenta).

Preheat the oven to 130°C (250°F/Gas 1). Carefully remove all the bones from the cod. You can keep the skin which helps to bind the sauce. Cut the fish into pieces about 6 x 6 cm (2½ x 2½ inches) and dry them with paper towels. Desalt the anchovies (rinse briefly under cold water) and remove the bones.

Sauté the onions gently until translucent in a saucepan in the oil, then add the garlic and anchovies and melt them into the oil, crushing them with a fork. Off the heat, add the parsley, milk and parmesan and mix well. Taste before seasoning with salt.

Flour the pieces of cod, shake off the excess, and arrange them in a single layer in an oiled baking dish. Cover with the sauce. Bake the dish uncovered for 3-4 hours. If the top dries out, add more milk, but never stir! You can also cook the cod on top of the stove, covered, for 2-4 hours on low heat without mixing but shaking the pot instead. It will be even better if it is baked for 3 hours one day and 1 hour the next day. Serve hot with white or yellow polenta.

* See page 11 for how to prepare dried or salted cod.

SEPPIE AL NERO E POLENTA

CUTTLEFISH IN INK & POLENTA

In Venice and throughout the region, it is customary to cook cuttlefish with its ink. It gives an incredible colour to the dish and a great deal of flavour. In September and October, you will find delicious baby cuttlefish!

SERVES 6 PREPARATION TIME: 30 MINUTES
COOKING TIME: 20 TO 60 MINUTES

1.4 kg (3 lb 2 oz) cuttlefish or squid
3 tablespoons olive oil
1 onion, chopped
2 garlic cloves, halved
2 tablespoons chopped flat-leaf (Italian) parsley
185 ml (6 fl oz/¾ cup) white wine
310 ml (10¾ fl oz/1¼ cups) vegetable stock, or water

THE POLENTA
1 litre (35 fl oz/4 cups) water
1½ teaspoons coarse salt
250 g (9 oz) polenta (cornmeal) (white or yellow)

Clean the cuttlefish, pulling out their insides gently so as not to break the ink sacs. Remove the beak and eyes and set the sacs aside. Cut the cuttlefish into strips. Heat the olive oil in a heavy-based saucepan and sauté the onion gently until translucent. Add the garlic and 1 tablespoon of the parsley Add the cuttlefish and stir for 2 minutes. Add the white wine and boil for 30 seconds. Next add some vegetable stock or water to cover the cuttlefish. Cook on medium heat uncovered for 20–40 minutes: the cuttlefish are cooked when they are tender.

To make the polenta: Bring the water to the boil, add the salt, then add the polenta in a stream and whisk for 2–3 minutes to prevent lumps from forming (follow the instructions on the packet). Stir frequently. The polenta should be quite liquid, if not, gradually add more boiling water. Cook for about 1 hour (or according to packet instructions if you are using a quick-cooking polenta).

Two minutes before the cuttlefish have finished cooking, add the ink. Taste and add salt if necessary. Sprinkle with the remaining parsley and serve with the polenta.

VARIATION

If you like, you can add 250 g (9 oz) fresh peas, briefly blanched.

TIP

If you can't find cuttlefish with their ink, you can buy ink from your fishmonger. Allow 16–24 g (½–1 oz).

FRITTO MISTO
MIXED FRIED SEAFOOD & VEGETABLES

In Venice, we can't resist a good seafood frittura! The mix is made up of fish, molluscs and crustaceans that vary according to the season, the market and the taste of the chef. It's even better with a few slices of fried eggplant, capsicum, zucchini, onion and leek, like the version served at Anice Stellato.

SERVES 6 PREPARATION TIME: 40 MINUTES COOKING TIME: 15 MINUTES

6 small whole red mullet
6 small whole sole, or other flat fish
300 g (10½ oz) small oily fish (such as sardines, fresh anchovies etc)
6 raw gamba prawns (shrimp), or other large variety of your choosing
12 small squid, cleaned*
300 g (10½ oz) scallops
2 litres (70 fl oz/8 cups) vegetable oil, for deep-frying
400 g (14 oz/2⅔ cups) plain (all-purpose) flour
1 capsicum (pepper), cut into strips
2 zucchini (courgettes), sliced into 1 cm (½ inch) rounds
1 eggplant (aubergine), cut into 1 cm (½ inch) semicircles
1 leek, pale part only, cut into strips
1 large red onion, sliced into rounds
Fleur de sel (fine sea salt)

THE VEGETABLE BATTER
100 g (3½ oz/⅔ cup) plain (all-purpose) flour
150-200 ml (5-7 fl oz) iced soda water

To make the vegetable batter: Combine the flour and enough soda water to make a thin batter. Set aside in the refrigerator.

Gut and remove the heads of the mullet and sole. Clean all the fish well. Peel the prawns. Cut the squid into rings. Clean the scallops. Drop the fish, prawns, squid and scallops into iced water to (4°C/39°F) to chill. In a deep-fryer or large heavy-based saucepan, heat the frying oil to 180°C (350°F), or until a cube of bread dropped into the oil turns golden brown in 15 seconds. Flour the fish and tap off the excess. Fry the largest fish first in the oil until golden brown, then remove and add, in turn, the smaller fish, squid, prawns then scallops. As soon as each is cooked, remove and drain on paper towels.

Dip the vegetables separately in the chilled batter, drain, then deep-fry them in the oil until they are golden brown.

Season the fish and vegetables with salt and serve immediately.

NOTE

It is important for the seafood to be very cold when added to the frying oil: it's this thermal shock that gives lightness to the dish!

* See page 80 for how to prepare squid.

ANGUILLA ALLA GRIGLIA

VENETIAN-STYLE GRILLED EEL

In Venice, eel is called bisato and it is caught in the brackish waters of the lagoon or in the wetland marshes of Comacchio. It is very good and the version at the restaurant Vini da Gigio is served simply grilled.

SERVES 6 PREPARATION TIME: 10 MINUTES COOKING TIME: 10 MINUTES

1.5 kg (3 lb 5 oz) small eels
Coarse salt or vinegar
Olive oil
1 tablespoon chopped flat-leaf (Italian) parsley
1 lemon

Ask the fishmonger to prepare and cut up the eels. Otherwise, I suggest you wear gloves and rub the eels with a handful of salt or vinegar to remove their slimy membrane. Gut them and cut into sections about 15 cm (6 inches) long. Wash and dry the pieces. Cut each piece in half lengthways. Oil the skin side of the eels and place them on a hotplate grill, cook on medium heat for about 10 minutes, or until their fat renders and they become crispy. Season with salt and pepper, sprinkle with parsley and serve with a wedge of lemon and polenta.

VARIATION: BISATO SU L'ARA (MURANO-STYLE EEL)

This is a typical dish from Murano, an island in the lagoon that's famous for its blown glass. It was traditional to place a pot of eel on the still-hot stone of the oven used to temper the glass vases, and let it cook gently ... Today eel is considered a great delicacy by Venetians. Heat 2 tablespoons of oil in a saucepan with the garlic, add about 20 fresh bay leaves and the eel cut into pieces about 5 cm (2 inches) long. Season with salt. Pour in 185 ml (6 fl oz/¾ cup) of water and 185 ml (6 fl oz/¾ cup) white wine vinegar. Cover and let it cook for about 15 minutes on low heat. Season with pepper. The oily meat of the eel will make an excellent sauce for the polenta to soak up!

FILETTI DI SOGLIOLA E CARCIOFI

FILLETS OF SOLE WITH ARTICHOKE

Sole, also called sfogi in Venice, is eaten a great deal in Veneto as those from the Adriatic are especially tasty.

SERVES 6 PREPARATION TIME: 30 MINUTES COOKING TIME: 20 MINUTES

6 small sole, 250 g (9 oz) each, or use john dory or flathead
1 onion, chopped
3 tablespoons olive oil
1 small handful of flat-leaf (Italian) parsley
1 large thyme sprig
Zest of 1 organic lemon
125 ml (4 fl oz/½ cup) dry white wine
Freshly ground black pepper
30 g (1 oz) butter
Sautéed artichokes to serve with the sole (see page 204)

Ask the fishmonger to skin and fillet the sole. Keep the trimmings to make a concentrated stock. Sauté the onion gently until translucent in a saucepan with 1 tablespoon of the oil, add the fish trimmings, parsley, thyme and lemon zest and stir. Add the white wine and boil for 30 seconds. Add 500 ml (17 fl oz/2 cups) water and let it reduce until you have 125 ml (4 fl oz/½ cup) liquid. Season with salt and pepper. Strain the liquid.

Rinse the sole fillets and pat dry on paper towels. Roll up the fillets in pairs to make 6 portions and secure with toothpicks. Heat the remaining oil and the butter in a large frying pan. Brown the fillets on medium heat, 2 minutes on each side. Add the reduced fish stock, cover and reduce on low heat for a few minutes. Serve topped with sautéed artichokes and spoon around the cooking juices.

ROMBO ALLE ERBE

TURBOT WITH HERBS

*You can find small 300 g (10½ oz) turbot for one like the
one I ate at Anice Stellato ... otherwise, allow one large 2 kg
(4 lb 8 oz) turbot for 6 people (allow for 50% wastage).*

SERVES 6 PREPARATION TIME: 20 MINUTES COOKING TIME: 40 MINUTES

2 kg (4 lb 8 oz) whole turbot
6 all-purpose potatoes, cut into 1.5 cm (⅝ inch) thick slices
80 ml (2½ fl oz/⅓ cup) olive oil
1 handful of thyme, chopped
1 handful of flat-leaf (Italian) parsley, chopped
20 g (¾ oz) butter
125 ml (4 fl oz/½ cup) white wine
1 onion, thinly sliced
200 g (7 oz) cherry tomatoes

Preheat the oven to 180°C (350°F/Gas 4). Ask your fishmonger to clean the
turbot. Rinse the fish, pat it dry with paper towels and brush with oil. Coat
the potato with oil, sprinkle with salt and place on a baking tray lined with
baking paper, sprinkle with the herbs and place the turbot on top, dark skin
side downwards. Top with a few thin slices of butter, season with salt and
bake for 10 minutes in the oven. Pour the white wine over the fish, scatter
over the onion rings and return it to the oven for about 30 minutes. Add
the cherry tomatoes 5 minutes before the end of the cooking time.

VARIATION: TURBOT FILLETS

Ask your fishmonger to fillet the turbot. Preheat the oven to 200°C
(400°F/Gas 6). Lay the fillets in an oiled baking dish, season with salt and
pepper and place in the oven. After 5 minutes of cooking, pour over 125 ml
(4 fl oz/½ cup) of white wine and cook for another 5 minutes. Keep the
turbot fillets warm. Add the juice of half a lemon, 2 tablespoons of olive oil
and 1 teaspoon of chopped parsley to the cooking juices. Reduce for a few
minutes and serve the fillets with the reduced juices and some vegetables.

ORATA AL FORNO

BAKED SEA BREAM

*The ideal for this dish is to buy small individual gilthead sea bream.
When a fish such as sea bream, sea bass or red mullet is cooked whole,
it's better to keep the scales on to prevent the juices from escaping.
To form a crust on the outside, dip the fish in breadcrumbs!*

SERVES 6 PREPARATION TIME: 30 MINUTES COOKING TIME: 40 MINUTES

12 small purple artichokes
125 ml (4 fl oz/½ cup) olive oil
1 garlic clove
1 tablespoon chopped flat-leaf (Italian) parsley
2½ tablespoons white wine
2½ tablespoons vegetable stock, or water
6 or 12 small sea bream (depending on size)
1 handful of flat-leaf (Italian) parsley sprigs
200 g (7 oz) home-made breadcrumbs

Preheat the oven to 200°C (400°F/Gas 6). Trim the artichokes as explained
on page 200, then cut in half. Heat 3 tablespoons of the oil in a saucepan
with the garlic (which is removed after cooking) and half the parsley. Place
the artichokes in the saucepan, cut side down, sauté them on high heat for
2–3 minutes, then add the white wine. After 2 minutes, add the stock, season
with salt, cover and cook for another 10–15 minutes on low heat, turning the
artichokes once. Add the rest of the parsley and some stock, if needed.

Ask your fishmonger to clean the sea bream but don't have them scaled. Season
them with salt inside and stuff them with the parsley sprigs. Dip them in the
breadcrumbs. Oil a hotplate or frying pan with the remaining oil. When it's hot,
brown the sea bream for 2 minutes on each side. Transfer the fish to a baking
dish and bake for 5 minutes in the oven. Serve with the braised artichokes.

NOTE

To cook sea bream, allow 10 minutes cooking time per 2.5 cm (1 inch) of thickness.

FILETTO DI BRANZINO E FINOCCHI

SEA BASS & FENNEL

*Called 'sea wolf' by people along the Mediterranean because of its voracity
and branzino or spigola by the Italians, sea bass is a typical fish of the
Adriatic, the whole Mediterranean and the Western Atlantic. It is enjoyed
for its firm, delicate and lean flesh. Fished throughout the year, it has
more flavour in the winter months. It works particularly well with fennel.*

SERVES 6 PREPARATION TIME: 15 MINUTES COOKING TIME: 15 MINUTES

3 sea bass, 600–700 g (1 lb 5 oz–1 lb 9 oz) each, or use barramundi
4 fennel bulbs, tough outer layer removed, thinly sliced
80 ml (2½ fl oz/⅓ cup) olive oil
1 tablespoon balsamic vinegar
1 handful of flat-leaf (Italian) parsley leaves, chopped

Preheat the oven to 180°C (350°F/Gas 4). Ask the fishmonger to fillet the fish.
Rinse the fillets and pat dry with paper towels. Pan-fry the fennel on medium heat
for 5 minutes in 2 tablespoons of the oil: they should stay crisp. Sprinkle with the
balsamic vinegar, stir for a few moments and season with salt and pepper. Oil
the fish fillets and place them skin side down on a baking tray lined with baking
paper. Place in the oven and cook for about 10 minutes. Season with salt. Serve
the sea bass fillets with the pan-fried fennel and sprinkle with the parsley.

CODA DI ROSPO ALLA GRIGLIA

GRILLED MONKFISH TAIL

The monkfish from the Adriatic Sea has a very delicate flavour. Look for firm and shiny flesh when buying. There's nothing better for appreciating this fish than a drizzle of olive oil and a squeeze of lemon juice. Use the head to make a stock: it is excellent!

<u>SERVES</u> 6 <u>PREPARATION TIME</u>: 10 MINUTES
<u>COOKING TIME</u>: 10 TO 20 MINUTES

6 small monkfish tails, about 180–200 g (6½–7 oz) each, or use stargazer
Olive oil
20 green asparagus spears, or other seasonal vegetables
1 tablespoon chopped flat-leaf (Italian) parsley
Juice of 1 lemon
Freshly ground black pepper

Remove the skin from the fish tails, rinse the tails and pat dry with paper towels. Make an incision along the central spine. Heat a hotplate or grill pan. Oil the fish tails and cook them for about 5 minutes on each side on medium heat. Lightly season with salt. Meanwhile, wash the asparagus, discard the bottom 3 cm (1¼ inches) of the spears (the tough section), cook them in a little boiling salted water for 5 minutes then pan-fry in a little olive oil for about 5 minutes. Check whether they're cooked with the point of a knife.

To make the sauce: Dissolve 4 pinches of salt into the lemon juice by mixing with a fork. Add 100 ml (3½ fl oz) olive oil, 2–3 turns of the pepper mill and the parsley. Serve the fish with the asparagus and a drizzle of sauce on top.

OVEN-BAKED VERSION FOR ONE LARGE MONKFISH

Preheat the oven to 180°C (350°F/Gas 4). Oil a baking dish, lay the monkfish tail in it and cover with parsley sprigs, drizzle over some olive oil and season with salt. Place in the oven. After 5 minutes, pour over 125 ml (4 fl oz/½ cup) of dry white wine (or fish stock made with the head of the monkfish) and cook for about 20 minutes, basting the monkfish with the juices once or twice.

FILETTO DI SAN PIETRO E FUNGHI

JOHN DORY WITH MUSHROOMS

John dory ('Saint Peter' in Italian) is a fish from the Adriatic that's highly prized for its firm and tasty flesh. It's recognised by its oval, flattened shape but above all by the black spot on each side, which according to legend are the marks of the Apostle Peter's thumb and forefinger …

SERVES 6 PREPARATION TIME: 15 MINUTES COOKING TIME: 25 MINUTES

500 g (1 lb 2 oz) wild mushrooms, or mixed mushrooms
3 tablespoons olive oil
1 garlic clove, halved
1 rosemary stalk
1.2 kg (2 lb 10 oz) john dory fillets
Plain (all-purpose) flour
40 g (1½ oz) butter

Preheat the oven to 200°C (400°F/Gas 6). To clean the mushrooms, immerse them in water twice, remove immediately and wipe dry. Cut the largest ones into two or three pieces. Heat 2 tablespoons of the oil in a frying pan with the garlic and rosemary on medium heat. Pan-fry the different mushrooms separately, stirring occasionally, for 5 minutes and season with salt and pepper. Lightly flour the fish fillets, season them with salt and pan-fry them in the butter and the remaining oil on medium heat for 2 minutes on each side. Place the mushrooms in the bottom of an oiled baking dish, lay the fish fillets on top and bake for about 4 minutes.

SUMMERTIME VERSION: CARLINA'S WAY

Carlina is the daughter of Giuseppe Cipriani, the owner of the legendary Harry's Bar in Venice. Preheat the oven to 200°C (400°F/Gas 6). Flour the fillets and cook them for 2 minutes on each side in a little butter and olive oil. Lay them in a buttered dish. Sprinkle over 2 tablespoons rinsed and chopped capers, 4 peeled and chopped tomatoes, the juice of 1 lemon and 30 g (1 oz) butter, cut into pieces. Bake for 4 minutes.

NOTE

Allow about 400–500 g (14 oz–1 lb 2 oz) gross weight per person (there's a lot of wastage!). Like turbot, john dory is cooked whole or as fillets.

SANTA CROCE, DORSODURO & GIUDECCA

When you get off the Riva di Biasio or San Stae vaporetto (coming from the Rialto, next to the Cà Pesaro museum), go south towards the old San Giacomo dell'Orio church. Don't miss its beautiful Gothic wooden ceiling that looks like the hull of a boat.

Stop in the welcoming Campo San Giacomo dell'Orio, with its greenery and surrounding cafés. At the **Al Prosecco (1)** *enoteca* you can feast on *cicheti* or buy regional wines.

Feel like an artisan gelato? Take Ruga Bella, cross the Campo Nazario Sauro and in Calle dei Bari you will find **Alaska (2)** *gelateria*. Ice-cream maker Carlo Pistacchi offers quality and originality ... In summer, put your money on the granitas made with real lemon juice!

Go back to Calle Larga, cross the Ponte del Megio and you will come to **La Zucca (3)**. This restaurant is a safe investment. Managed since 1981 by Rudy, you can enjoy vegetarian dishes there as well as traditional Venetian meat dishes made from tripe, veal tongue or rabbit. They offer a wide selection of vegetables. Their pumpkin flan alone is worth the trip. Make sure you book!

ROUTE 2

Head to San Tomà on foot or by vaporetto to visit the Scuola Grande di San Giovanni Evangelista. This confraternity is one of the oldest in Venice (1261). In Calle San Pantalon is the **Tonolo (4)** *pasticceria* (my favourite pâtisserie in Venice). Tonolo is a compulsory stop for a coffee (standing at the counter) and a pastry. I love their *bignè* (choux puffs) filled with zabaione, the *meringhe* (soft meringues filled with whipped cream), the *cannoncini* (puff pastry rolled into a cannon shape and filled with cream) and, of course, the *fritole* and *crostoli* during *Carnevale*! Heading south you come to the great **Campo Santa Margherita (5)**, where Venetians meet to have a drink, standing up or sitting comfortably on the bar terraces (go to Il Caffè, and for a *cicheto* there's La Bifora). This Campo is one of the few places in Venice (along with the Fondamenta Ormesini and Misericordia) where there's a bit of life at night! During the day, you will also find fruit and vegetable *bancarelle* (stalls) and fish *bancarelle*, including the one owned by Il Signor Silvano.

For other gastronomic discoveries, continue towards Campo San Barnaba after the Ponte dei Pugni. At the quay, **Barca (6)**, a superb boat filled with magnificent fruits and vegetables awaits you!

Campo San Barnaba: a visit to the **Pantagruelica (7)** food store is imperative. Sommelier Maurizio and his wife Silvia offer the best regional products, wines and rare alcohols ... They know all the producers! There you will find the finest hand-made pastas, reserve hams cured for 36 months,

Montegalda goat cheeses, Sartorelli biscuits, and Orto, the wine of Venice ...

Go to **Grom (8)** *gelateria* in the same Campo and enjoy an ice-cream cone with the flavours of the season. Take Calle San Barnaba, where you will find friendly little family *trattorias* that serve traditional regional cooking. **La Bitta (9)**, for example, specialises in meat (in the evening), and **La Furatola (10)** in fish from the Adriatic. For a *focaccia veneziana*, the classic Venetian brioche-style cake, go to **Nonno Colussi's** *pasticceria* **(11)** in Calle San Barnaba. Franco Colussi, nicknamed 'Nonno' (grandpa), will explain how his *focaccia* takes 30 hours to make, including 3 for rising and 2 for kneading! If you're lucky, you can admire a multitude of *foccace* hanging from the ceiling! Call to find out his opening hours, which change according to his mood.

From Campo San Barnaba, head towards the Fondamenta and the Calle de la Toletta. You can stop at **Ai Artisti (12)** wine bar and *osteria* for a midday aperitif or even have lunch there after a tour of the bookstores in the area.

ROUTE 3

To relax and fully appreciate the view of the Giudecca canal, there's nothing better than sitting on the terrace of **Gelati Nico (13)** on the Fondamenta Zattere dei Gesuati and enjoying a *gianduiotto*, a slice of gianduja ice-cream drowned in whipped cream! For a *cicheto* or to buy some wine, on the Fondamenta opposite the church of San Trovaso you'll find **Cantinone-Già Schiavi (14)**, an historical institution where *mamma* Alessandra makes her famous rustic *cicheti* 'live' behind the counter. Every Venetian knows this place ... You could also decide to eat in a lovely location on the Fondamenta Zattere, such as **La Riviera (15)**, with its beautiful terrace facing Giudecca and the Molino Stucky.

If you are looking for a little peace and quiet, go and discover the island of Giudecca. This is an island in the lagoon opposite the Zattere, away from the tourist trail. Take the vaporetto and get off at Palanca, then go left and turn into Calle delle Erbe. Stop at the *trattoria* **Altanella (16)**. You will be welcomed by the fourth-generation owners! In the family atmosphere, Roberto presides over the dining room while his brother Stefano is in the kitchen. I ate the best cuttlefish ink gnocchi of my life there! The rooms are lovely and the terrace is charming, it feels like you're in the country.

Near the Palanca vaporetto stop you can do your fish shopping at **Fabio Gavagnin's fishmongers (17)**. He will give you good advice, with a smile! For bread and grissini, stop at the bakery **Il Panificio Claudio Crosara (18)**, opposite the beautiful Gesuati church on the other side of the canal, which is reflected in the window. Finally, stop at **Fortuny (19)** for some beautiful arts and fabrics.

ANARA COL PIEN

STUFFED DUCK

Stuffed roast duck is one of the traditional dishes of the great Festa del Redentore which is held on the third Sunday in July. This recipe is inspired by a dish I enjoyed at the Vini da Gigio restaurant.

SERVES 6   PREPARATION TIME: 30 MINUTES   COOKING TIME: 1¼ HOURS

2 x 2 kg (4 lb 8 oz) ducks

THE STUFFING
1 onion, finely chopped
1 carrot, finely chopped
1 celery stalk, finely chopped
1 garlic clove, finely chopped
A few sage leaves, finely chopped
A few thyme and marjoram leaves, finely chopped
1 handful of flat-leaf (Italian) parsley, finely chopped
1 rosemary stalk, finely chopped
The liver and heart of the duck
150 g (5½ oz) sopressa (Venetian salami), or pancetta or bacon, chopped
Grated zest of 1 lemon
70 g (2½ oz) parmesan cheese, grated
1 egg
Home-made breadcrumbs

THE SAUCE
1 onion, diced
1 carrot, diced
1 celery stalk, diced
2 garlic cloves
1 bay leaf
1 rosemary stalk
A few sage leaves
2 tablespoons olive oil
125 ml (4 fl oz/½ cup) dry white wine
1 litre (35 fl oz/4 cups) beef stock (preferably home-made,
   otherwise use an organic stock cube)

To make the stuffing: Combine the onion, carrot, celery, garlic and herbs, mix them with the chopped liver, heart and sopressa, add the lemon zest, parmesan and egg and season with salt and pepper. Add enough breadcrumbs to make a fairly firm stuffing and use it to stuff the duck. Tie up the duck with kitchen string.

To make the sauce: In a cast-iron pot or large deep frypan, large enough to hold the ducks, sauté the onion, carrot, celery, garlic and herbs in the oil on medium heat. After 2 minutes, add the ducks and brown them in the oil. Season with salt. Add the wine and let it bubble for a few minutes. Add the stock, bring it to the boil, cover and let the ducks simmer for about 1 hour. Preheat the oven to 180°C (350°F/Gas 4).

Remove the ducks from the liquid, transfer to a baking dish and bake for 15 minutes. Meanwhile, reduce the cooking juices on medium heat with the vegetables and then remove the herbs and process in a food processor to make a smooth sauce. Cut the string from the ducks and take out the stuffing, cut the ducks into pieces and spoon over the sauce. Serve with polenta and/or roast potatoes.

OCA 'ROSTA

ROAST GOOSE WITH APPLES & CHESTNUTS

*A typical autumn meat in Veneto, goose is a legacy of the
Jewish community, established in Venice since the eleventh
century, which uses it extensively in its cooking.*

SERVES 8 PREPARATION TIME: 10 MINUTES COOKING TIME: 3¼ HOURS

1 goose—5 kg (10 lb 16 oz) net weight, plus giblets
1 teaspoon ground cinnamon
4 pinches of freshly grated nutmeg
2 cloves
1.5 kg (3 lb 5 oz) reinette apples, or other apple that holds its shape
   e.g. golden delicious, peeled, cored and cut into large segments
500 g (1 lb 2 oz) cooked chestnuts (can be purchased in packets)
2-3 handfuls of stale breadcrumbs
185 ml (6 fl oz/¾ cup) dry white wine

Preheat the oven to 180°C (350°F/Gas 4). Clean the goose, reserving the
giblets and excess fat. Chop the giblets and mix them with the spices, half
the apple and half the chestnuts. Add the stale breadcrumbs and season
with salt and pepper. Season the inside of the goose with salt, stuff it three-
quarters full with the stuffing mixture and sew up the opening with kitchen
string. Render the goose fat in a flameproof casserole dish and brown the
goose on all sides on low heat for 10 minutes, then pour over the wine
and let it evaporate. Cover with a sheet of foil and bake for 30 minutes.
Continue to cook the goose uncovered for about 2½ hours, regularly
basting the goose with its juices: the skin should be crisp and golden.

Sauté the remaining apple in a frying pan on low heat in a little goose fat, stirring
often, until it is tender. Reheat the remaining chestnuts in another frying pan.

Degrease the goose's cooking juices by cooling them or placing some paper
towels on the surface to absorb the fat. Serve the goose on a platter surrounded
by apples and chestnuts. Cut into 8 pieces, slice the stuffing and drizzle with the
cooking juices.

NOTE

To cook the goose (cleaned), allow 1 hour's baking time per kilo, net weight.

VARIATION

In Treviso, roast goose is traditionally served with raw celery: *oca col sedano*. I still
remember its aroma from when I was little, at the *Fiere di San Luca* (Fair of Saint
Luke) held in October.

FARAONA ARROSTA E SALSA PEVERADA

ROAST GUINEA FOWL WITH PEVERADA SAUCE

Poultry is very popular in Veneto. As for the peverada sauce, a recipe for it is found in the first recipe book of dishes from Veneto written in the fourteenth century. It also goes very well with rabbit and game. Choose a free-range guinea fowl raised outdoors, its meat will be darker and tastier, similar to pheasant. It is cooked like chicken.

SERVES 4 PREPARATION TIME: 30 MINUTES
COOKING TIME: 1 HOUR 10 MINUTES

6 sage leaves
2 rosemary stalks
3 garlic cloves, halved
100 g (3½ oz) pancetta or bacon, thinly sliced
1 large guinea fowl
2 tablespoons olive oil
125 ml (4 fl oz/½ cup) dry white wine

THE PEVERADA SAUCE
200 g (7 oz) chicken livers + the livers from the guinea fowl
185 ml (6 fl oz/¾ cup) olive oil
2 garlic cloves
Zest and juice of 1–2 lemons
100 g (3½ oz) sopressa (Venetian salami), or 8 anchovy fillets, chopped
60 g (2¼ oz) capers, rinsed and chopped
1 bunch of flat-leaf (Italian) parsley, chopped

Preheat the oven to 200°C (400°F/Gas 6). Put a couple of sage leaves, a small rosemary stalk, 1 garlic clove and a slice of pancetta inside the guinea fowl and cover the fowl with thin slices of pancetta tied on with kitchen string. Heat the oil in a flameproof casserole dish on medium-high heat, add the remaining garlic, sage, rosemary and the guinea fowl and brown on all sides. Add the wine and let it bubble for 1 minute, season with salt and pepper and bake in the oven for about 40 minutes, regularly basting the fowl with its juices.

To make the sauce: Clean the chicken and guinea fowl livers and chop them finely with a knife or in a food processor. In a saucepan, heat the oil with a garlic clove (remove it when the oil is very hot) and the lemon zest, then the sopressa (or anchovies), capers and chopped liver and cook on low heat for about 10 minutes, stirring. At the end of the cooking time, add the lemon juice, season generously with pepper, and add the parsley. Leave on low heat for a few more minutes, then turn off the heat. Cut the guinea fowl into 4 pieces, serve on a dish and pour over the sauce, or serve on a bed of Savoy cabbage (see page 214).

VARIATION
You can replace the lemon juice with wine vinegar, increasing the quantities slightly, which will result in a more acidic sauce.

POLLO IN TECIA

PAN-ROASTED CHICKEN

This is a humble dish that's very common in Veneto. Poultry and rabbits have always been kept on the land of the lagoon. Chicken was the Sunday meal of our great-grandparents, and also of my childhood. This ruspante (free-range) chicken is served roasted with potatoes or polenta to mop up all the juices!

<u>SERVES</u> 6 <u>PREPARATION TIME</u>: 20 MINUTES <u>COOKING TIME</u>: 1 HOUR

1 large free-range chicken, cut into 8 pieces
80 ml (2½ fl oz/⅓ cup) olive oil
1 onion, chopped
50 g (1¾ oz) pancetta, chopped
2 garlic cloves, unpeeled
2 celery stalks, chopped
2 rosemary stalks
10 sage leaves
80 ml (2½ fl oz/⅓ cup) white wine
185 ml (6 fl oz/¾ cup) hot home-made vegetable stock, or use an organic stock cube

THE POTATOES
2½ tablespoons olive oil
1 onion, chopped
1 garlic clove, halved
2 rosemary stalks
1 kg (2 lb 4 oz) potatoes, washed, dried and cut into small chunks

Brown the chicken pieces on high heat in a large cast-iron pot with 2 tablespoons of oil (you can drain off the fat). Set aside. Sauté the onion in the same pot with the remaining oil on medium heat and add the pancetta, garlic, celery, the herbs and chicken pieces. Season with salt and pepper. Add the white wine and let it evaporate for a few minutes. Add the hot stock and lower the heat. Simmer covered for 40 minutes on medium heat (take out the chicken breasts after 20 minutes). Keep the chicken warm and reduce the sauce on low heat before serving.

To make the potatoes: Heat the oil on medium heat in a large frying pan with the chopped onion, garlic and rosemary. Sauté for 3 minutes. Add the potato and cook for 20 minutes on medium heat, stirring frequently. Season with salt. Serve the chicken on the potato.

<u>VARIATION: CHICKEN WITH TOMATO</u>

Add a 300 g (10½ oz) tin of peeled tomatoes, a good Italian brand such as San Marzano, and reduce the amount of stock.

CONIGLIO IN PENTOLA AL POMODORO

BRAISED RABBIT WITH TOMATO

Rabbit is cooked a great deal in Veneto. You can marinate the rabbit the day before in a mixture of half water and half vinegar. Choose a rabbit with pale pink meat, its fat should be white.

SERVES 6 PREPARATION TIME: 20 MINUTES COOKING TIME: 1 HOUR

1 rabbit cut into 6 pieces + 2 thighs
1 onion, finely chopped
1 carrot, finely chopped
1 celery stalk, finely chopped
80 ml (2½ fl oz/⅓ cup) olive oil
2 garlic cloves, halved
2 rosemary stalks
185 ml (6 fl oz/¾ cup) dry white wine
600 g (1 lb 5 oz) tomatoes, peeled (see note page 96)
1 bunch of basil, leaves only, torn
The liver of the rabbit

Wash and dry the rabbit. Sauté the onion, carrot and celery in a heavy-based saucepan in 2 tablespoons of the oil on medium heat and set aside. In the same pan, heat the remaining oil on high heat, add the rabbit pieces and thighs with the garlic and rosemary and brown them on both sides. Add the wine and let it evaporate for 2 minutes then add the tomatoes and basil. Cook, covered, on low heat: remove the saddles after 20 minutes and continue cooking the thighs for another 30 minutes. You can add the liver of the rabbit, chopped, 5 minutes before the end of the cooking time. Remove the garlic and serve with polenta or good bread.

OVEN-BAKED VERSION

A variation on this classic recipe is to cook the rabbit in the oven without the tomato. It is replaced with 500 ml (17 fl oz/2 cups) of chicken stock.

BOLLITO MISTO

VENETIAN POT-AU-FEU

This dish is also called carne lessa (boiled meat). It's a traditional dish enjoyed at Christmas or on festival holidays, and is served in all good Venetian restaurants from autumn to spring. This pot-au-feu is traditionally presented on a trolley. The pieces of meat are kept warm in the stock and cut to order. The pot-au-feu below is served with three condiments. It's real theatre!

SERVES 8 PREPARATION TIME: 30 MINUTES COOKING TIME: 3¼ HOURS

3 carrots, chopped
4 celery stalks, chopped
3 onions, studded with cloves
1 marrowbone
A few peppercorns
A handful of flat-leaf (Italian) parsley stalks
2 bay leaves
1 kg (2 lb 4 oz) blade or braising beef
500 g (1 lb 2 oz) breast of veal
1 large free-range chicken, or capon
1 *musetto* or 1 *cotechino*, or other suitable sausage (see page 182)
30 g (1 oz) coarse salt
Mostarda (candied fruit with mustard oil, available from
 delicatessens, ask for the Lazzaris brand)
Horseradish sauce (see page 188)

SALSA VERDE
50 g (1¾ oz) crustless sandwich bread
125 ml (4 fl oz/½ cup) wine vinegar
50 g (1¾ oz) flat-leaf (Italian) parsley leaves
50 g (1¾ oz) celery leaves
50 g (1¾ oz) capers, rinsed
50 g (1¾ oz) cornichons
2 hard-boiled eggs
8 anchovy fillets
1 garlic clove
100 ml (3½ fl oz) olive oil

Pour 6 litres (210 fl oz/24 cups) of water into a large pot. Add the carrot, celery, onion, marrowbone, peppercorns, parsley and bay leaves. Bring to the boil, season with salt, add the beef and return to the boil. Lower the heat to the minimum setting, skim the broth several times, cover and simmer for 30 minutes. Add the veal breast and chicken and cook for 2½ hours, regularly skimming the broth. Cook the *cotechino* or *musetto* separately, 2 hours for fresh sausage, 15 minutes for precooked sausage (see page 182).

To make the *salsa verde*: Moisten the bread with the vinegar and let it soak for a few minutes. Put everything into a food processor, and process to make a salsa.

To serve, place the pot on the table, take out the meat and cut it up on a board in front of the dinner guests, then return it to the stock. Serve with coarse salt, *mostarda*, horseradish sauce and *salsa verde*.

MUSETTO E PURÉ
SAUSAGE & MASHED POTATOES

Musetto is a pork cooking sausage made from pork mince, pork rind and meat from the snout, hence its name ('nose'). It also contains spices. You can bring it back from Venice vacuum-packed. Alternatively you can use cotechino or zampone, which are more widely available (especially precooked and vacuum-packed). Both of these sausages have a similar taste to musetto, and the same gelatinous texture … that I do so love! Obviously, musetto is a winter dish, and it is also used in bollito misto (see page 180).

SERVES 6 PREPARATION TIME: 45 MINUTES
COOKING TIME: 2 HOURS (35 MINUTES WITH PRECOOKED SAUSAGES)

2 fresh *musetto* sausages, 600 g (1 lb 5 oz) each, or 2 *cotechini* or *zampone*

FOR THE MASHED POTATOES
1 kg (2 lb 4 oz) roasting potatoes
30 g (1 oz) butter
250–300 ml (9 fl oz–10½ fl oz/1–1¼ cups) hot milk
Freshly grated nutmeg

For precooked vacuum-packed sausages: Boil in water for 15 minutes in the packaging (check the cooking time on the package).

For fresh sausages: Prick them in several places with a fork to prevent them from bursting during cooking. Place the sausages in a large saucepan of cold water, bring to the boil and cook on low heat for 2 hours.

To make the mashed potatoes: Peel the potatoes, cut them into quarters and steam them for 20 minutes, or until you can easily insert the point of a knife. Alternatively, halve the potatoes and boil in water. Mash them while they're still hot using a potato masher or ricer. Add the butter in pieces and the hot milk as needed. Season with salt and nutmeg. Mix well until the mash is smooth.

Serve the hot sausage sliced on the mashed potatoes, or use polenta.

RECOMMENDATION

The key to a good mashed potato is to use floury (roasting) potatoes, mash them while they're still hot so they have the right texture and serve them immediately!

VARIATION

Mash the potatoes roughly and replace the butter and milk with a good-quality olive oil and salt.

MAIALE AL LATTE

PORK IN MILK

In the traditional recipe using pork loin, the meat is marinated in white wine before cooking to give it more flavour. It's also quite fine without the marinade. This recipe is inspired by my mother's version.

SERVES 6 PREPARATION TIME: 30 MINUTES COOKING TIME: 2 HOURS

1 litre (35 fl oz/4 cups) milk
2 garlic cloves, halved
10 sage leaves
2 rosemary stalks
Juice and zest of 1 lemon
1.2 kg (2 lb 10 oz) boned pork loin
2 tablespoons olive oil
20 g (¾ oz) butter

Heat the milk gently in a medium saucepan with the garlic, herbs and lemon zest. Brown the meat in a large saucepan on high heat with the oil and butter, drain off the excess fat, season with salt and pepper and pour over the hot milk mixture. Simmer covered for 1½ hours. Remove the meat from the saucepan and set aside. Add the lemon juice to the milk and let it reduce: the sauce will curdle from the acidity of the lemon. Remove the garlic and lemon zest and serve the meat covered with the sauce. Serve with seasonal vegetables.

VARIATION

Replace the milk with beer at room temperature, added gradually during cooking. Simmer meat and potatoes on a bed of onions braised with 1 tablespoon juniper berries and 1 teaspoon cumin seeds. This version with beer and potatoes comes to us via the Austrians who occupied Venice at the end of the eighteenth century after Napoleon.

FEGATO ALLA VENEZIANA

VENETIAN-STYLE LIVER

*This is a traditional dish inspired by one enjoyed at the restaurant
Antiche Carampane. Use calf liver, which is more delicate than
beef or pork liver. Keep a close eye on the liver, as it cooks very
quickly: it should be pink inside. If it's overcooked, it will be tough.
If it's undercooked, it may not appeal ... especially to Italians!*

SERVES 6 PREPARATION TIME: 20 MINUTES RESTING TIME: 1 HOUR
COOKING TIME: 35 MINUTES

750 g (1 lb 10 oz) calf liver
2 tablespoons white wine vinegar
80 ml (2½ fl oz/⅓ cup) olive oil
750 g (1 lb 10 oz) white onions, sliced into rings
20 g (¾ oz) butter
1 tablespoon chopped flat-leaf (Italian) parsley
Grilled polenta (cornmeal) (see page 194)

THE POLENTA
2 litres (70 fl oz/8 cups) water
2 teaspoons coarse salt
500 g (1 lb 1 oz/2⅔ cups) polenta (cornmeal)

To make the polenta: Bring the water to the boil, add the salt, then add the polenta
in a stream and whisk for 2-3 minutes to prevent lumps from forming (follow the
instructions on the packet). Stir frequently. The polenta should be quite liquid,
if not, gradually add more boiling water. Cook for about 1 hour (or according to
packet instructions if you are using a quick-cooking polenta). Allow the polenta to
set and grill as explained on page 194.

If possible, disgorge the liver for 1 hour in water with the vinegar. Before cooking,
remove the thin membrane covering the liver. Cut the liver into thin slices (about
3 mm/⅛ inch thick, 3-4 cm/1¼-1½ inches wide and 6-7 cm/2½-2¾ inches long).

Heat half the oil in a frying pan and gently cook the onion for about 30 minutes,
covered, adding a few tablespoons of water if necessary. Remove from the heat
when it is well cooked and translucent. Set aside. In the same frying pan, heat the
remaining oil on medium-high heat and fry the liver quickly on both sides. Allow
3 minutes cooking time overall—it should still be pink in the middle. Season with salt
and pepper. Combine the liver with the onions and butter. Sprinkle with parsley and
serve with grilled polenta.

VARIATION

Add pine nuts and raisins to the dish, rehydrated in water and vinegar. You can
also add fresh or rehydrated dried figs. In this case, cook them for 3 minutes with
the onion and sprinkle with lemon zest.

NOTE

Liver made the Venetian way, a popular dish throughout the Mediterranean, has
spread around the world. The recipe goes back to a distant time when it was
customary to soften the slightly bitter aftertaste of liver with a sweet ingredient.
The Romans and then the Byzantines served it with figs. Its Latin name, *jecor
ficatum* gave us *fegato* (liver).

LINGUA DI VITELLO

VEAL TONGUE

I enjoyed this dish at the restaurant La Zucca, served with a pumpkin flan and potatoes. The tongue was meltingly tender and delicious. Use the more delicate veal tongue rather than pork or beef tongue. Here is my recipe …

SERVES 6 PREPARATION TIME: 20 MINUTES RESTING TIME: 2 HOURS
COOKING TIME: 2 HOURS

1 veal tongue—1.5 kg (3 lb 5 oz)
1 celery stalk, roughly chopped
1 carrot, roughly chopped
1 onion, studded with a few cloves
1 handful of flat-leaf (Italian) parsley sprigs, stalks and leaves separated
2 bay leaves
1 teaspoon peppercorns
3 tablespoons olive oil

Soak the tongue in cold water for 2 hours. Change the water, bring to the boil in a saucepan and cook for 1 hour on low heat. Add the celery, carrot, onion, parsley stalks, bay leaves and peppercorns and continue cooking for 1 hour: the tongue should be tender. Let the tongue cool a little, then remove its skin and cut into slices about 1–1.5 cm (½–⅝ inch) thick. Purée the parsley leaves with the olive oil, salt and pepper. Serve the tongue warm with vegetable gratin, a green drizzle of parsley, salsa verde (see page 180), or horseradish sauce (see below).

HORSERADISH SAUCE

Grate a horseradish root and combine with some white vinegar and a pinch each of sugar, salt and pepper. It can be stored in a jar in the refrigerator. Otherwise, buy ready-made horseradish sauce.

NOTE

Tongue is part of a traditional *bollito misto* (see page 180) but it must be cooked separately because you don't use its cooking liquid. It is usually eaten with horseradish sauce (*cren*), a legacy of Austrian rule and adopted by Venetian cuisine from the nineteenth century. Beef tongue is mainly eaten *salmistrata*, in the Jewish style, which is to say brined with herbs, spices and nitrite salt. It's a fairly complicated recipe, and it's usually bought ready-made instead from the butcher or delicatessen.

TRIPPA AL SUGO

TRIPE IN TOMATO SAUCE

Here is a typical Veneto recipe for tripe. For an express tripe dish, I recommend buying precooked tripe. In France, you can buy tripe in terrine form in aspic and it can be prepared in 30 minutes. Uncooked tripe, pre-washed and blanched, can be bought from a tripe butcher (in Veneto, it's also available from the supermarket!) and needs to be cooked for 4–6 hours. Good quality tripe is fairly dark, not completely bleached.

SERVES 6 PREPARATION TIME: 15 MINUTES
COOKING TIME: 45 MINUTES (+ 4 HOURS IF USING UNCOOKED TRIPE)

1.5 kg (3 lb 5 oz) terrine of cooked tripe (preferably veal), or 900 g (2 lb) uncooked tripe
1 onion, finely chopped
1 celery stalk, finely chopped
1 carrot, finely chopped
50 g (1¾ oz) bacon, or unsmoked pancetta
2 tablespoons olive oil
Bouquet garni (with sage, bay leaf, flat-leaf (Italian) parsley and rosemary)
1 garlic clove, halved
300 g (10½ oz) tinned peeled tomatoes
250 ml (9 fl oz/1 cup) beef stock
Nutmeg for grating
100 g (3½ oz) parmesan cheese, grated

Ready-to-use tripe: Rinse under cold water and blanch for 5 minutes.

Uncooked tripe: Cook for at least 4 hours in boiling salted water.

Sweat the onion, celery, carrot and bacon in a heavy-based saucepan with the oil on low heat, add the bouquet garni, garlic and the tripe cut into 5 cm (2 inch) strips. Stir for 2 minutes, add some salt, the tomato and stock. Cover and cook for 30 minutes on low heat, stirring occasionally. Grate over the nutmeg (the equivalent of a pinch) and season with salt and pepper. At the end of the cooking time, sprinkle with parmesan and serve with soft polenta or slices of toasted country-style bread.

VARIATIONS

The basic recipe stays the same, but you can leave out the tomato, and/or make it into a soup by adding some good beef stock.

PROMENADE IN THE ISLANDS OF THE LAGOON, MAZZORBO AND BURANO

Make the most of a sunny day by taking the vaporetto at Fondamenta Nuove to Burano, the island in the lagoon with the brightly coloured houses (recognisable to fishermen on foggy days!). After a soothing and magical half-hour trip across the water, step off at Mazzorbo, connected to Burano by a pretty bridge. This island is devoted to the cultivation of vegetables and fruit trees, including grapevines, and fish farming.

You can discover its vegetable gardens by taking the public pathway around the Tenuta Venissa estate, which offers an historical picture of the peasant culture of the lagoon. You can admire the vineyard of the native *dorona* grape variety, grown over two hectares enclosed by an eighteenth-century wall, and enjoy its rare and precious Venissa wine, produced by the Bisol family. On the estate is a high-quality restaurant, **L'Ostello**, that takes the produce of the lagoon to the next level. It also offers well-priced rooms and a unique awakening in the lagoon.

For lunch or dinner in a traditional *trattoria*, cross the Tenuta Venissa vegetable garden and once over the bridge you're in Burano, the island known worldwide for its needle lace school.

Sample the local cuisine at **Al Gatto Nero**. Since 1965, chef Ruggero has treated us to traditional dishes made with the best local ingredients. Try the famous *risotto di go'* (a lagoon fish) or the home-made pasta with seafood specialities. There's a charming 1960s ambience and a pleasant terrace on the canal.

On the main square is another typical and popular eating place: **Da Romano**. Everyone knows it! Order a fish-based meal.

To visit on the island: The Lace Museum and San Martino church with its very, very crooked campanile!

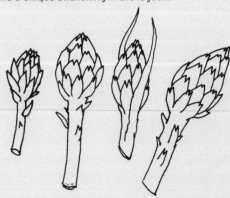

POLENTA

WHAT IS IT EXACTLY?

Polenta is a kind of cornmeal. Very popular in the northern regions of Italy, the cornmeal used for polenta can be more or less finely ground. Usually yellow, it can also be fine and white as in Veneto and Friuli. It needs to be cooked for a long time: 40 minutes to 1 hour—45 minutes is needed to make it properly digestible. If you don't have the time, you can buy quick-cooking polentas that are ready in 5 minutes. Nevertheless, I recommend you try traditional polenta cooked the old-fashioned way, as it has a much better taste and texture!

A LITTLE HISTORY

The corn for making polenta comes to us from the Americas. It was first grown in Veneto towards the end of the sixteenth century. For a long time this plant has enabled people to feed themselves, feed their livestock, warm themselves and fill their mattresses (with the dry corn husks). Polenta also has the advantage of being easier to make than bread! A rustic and convivial dish, polenta has the added benefit of being suitable for people with gluten allergies, as it doesn't contain any.

BASIC RECIPE

To cook polenta follow the instructions on the packet. Pour cooked polenta onto a wooden board or into a dish and allow to set before you grill or fry it.

HOW SHOULD IT BE SERVED AND WHAT WITH?

Grilled polenta: Polenta is served grilled as an aperitif snack with *baccalà mantecato* (see page 12), sausage (see page 40), meat or fish. To grill, cut cooked polenta into 1 cm (½ inch) slices and place them in a very hot frying pan or on baking paper under the oven grill. Sear on both sides.

Pan-fried polenta: Brown slices of cooked polenta in a little butter or olive oil.

Deep-fried polenta: Cut cooked polenta into sticks and deep-fry in oil. They're a replacement for chips!

Soft polenta: Soft polenta is eaten with small prawns (see page 84), cuttlefish in ink (see page 150), *baccalà alla vicentina* (see page 148), cheese such as Gorgonzola, or with fried mushrooms (see page 196). For dessert, it's found in the recipes for *zaletti* biscuits (see page 240) and *pinza* (see page 236).

THE RIGHT EQUIPMENT

The *paiolo* is the polenta pot. It is made of copper and has a rounded base. There is an electric version of the *paiolo* (for those who don't want to spend their time stirring!). You also need a large wooden spatula and a wooden board to pour the cooked polenta onto, otherwise you can use a dish or mould that will shape the polenta. At my home in Veneto, polenta is cut on a wooden board with kitchen string.

POLENTA E FUNGHI

POLENTA & MUSHROOMS

This is a typical autumn recipe, to serve as a side dish or with cured meats and cheeses. In Veneto, you can try the delicious chiodini, local mushrooms.

SERVES 8 PREPARATION TIME: 20 MINUTES COOKING TIME: 1 HOUR

500 g (1 lb 2 oz) polenta (cornmeal)
2 teaspoons coarse salt
1 kg (2 lb 4 oz) wild mushrooms, or mushrooms of your choice
3 tablespoons olive oil
1 garlic clove, halved
1 rosemary stalk

To make the polenta: For 500 g (1 lb 2 oz) polenta, use 4 times its volume in water (2 litres/70 fl oz/8 cups). Bring the water to the boil in a saucepan, add the coarse salt and quickly add the polenta in a stream, mixing at the same time with a large wooden spoon to avoid lumps. Be careful of splatter! For a more liquid polenta, add a little more boiling water at the start of the cooking. Stir frequently. Cook on a very low heat until the polenta comes away from the side of the pan. Allow about 1 hour to cook, covered (or according to packet instructions if you are using a quick-cooking polenta).

To clean the mushrooms, immerse them in water twice. Take them out immediately and wipe dry with paper towels. Cut the largest into two or three pieces and slice the porcini, if using. Heat 2 tablespoons of the oil in a frying pan with the garlic and rosemary. Add the mushrooms in batches and cook on high heat, without stirring, until the mushrooms have released their water. Season with salt and pepper and set aside. Combine all the mushrooms and cook for a further 5 minutes on low heat. Check the seasoning. Serve on the hot polenta.

NOTE

A thin crust will form on the base of the polenta pan by the end of the cooking time. Don't try to scrub it off! Soak the pan in water and the crust will come off by itself.

VARIATIONS

You can make a richer polenta by replacing half the water with milk, or by adding mascarpone cheese, or butter and parmesan cheese at the end of the cooking time.

POLENTA E SALSICCIA

POLENTA & SAUSAGES

A tasty and convivial dish, typical of autumn days.
Choose a traditionally made artisan sausage such as the
luganega di Treviso, flavoured with sweet spices ...

SERVES 6 PREPARATION TIME: 10 MINUTES
COOKING TIME: 1 HOUR 20 MINUTES

2 litres (70 fl oz/8 cups) water
20 g (¾ oz) coarse salt
500 g (1 lb 2 oz) polenta (cornmeal)
6 artisan sausages
185 ml (6 fl oz/¾ cup) white wine, or water

Preheat the oven to 200°C (400°F/Gas 6). Make the polenta as explained on
page 194. Once cooled, cut into 1 cm (½ inch) thick slices, lay them on some baking
paper and brown them for about 20 minutes in the oven turning halfway through.
Meanwhile, cook the sausages in a hot frying pan. Brown them first on low heat
on both sides, adding the white wine or water and seasoning only lightly, then
finish the cooking on high heat. Serve the sausages on the hot slices of polenta.

I CARCIOFI

ARTICHOKES

IL CARCIOFO VIOLETTO DI SANT'ERASMO
(THE PURPLE ARTICHOKE OF SANT'ERASMO)

Sant'Erasmo is an island in the lagoon that has been the vegetable garden of Venice since the sixteenth century. Its soil, lapped by the sea and the lagoon, gives a unique flavour to its naturally seasoned vegetables. The artichokes grown here are exceptional. Each artichoke plant produces one *castraura* ('cut') at the beginning of the season. This is a soft and fleshy bud that is picked before maturity. Four artichokes develop after that, the *botoli*, and then, after about 20 days, between 18 and 20 larger artichokes appear. In former times the *castraure* were reserved exclusively for the *Doge*.

ITALIAN VARIETIES

Each region of Italy has its own variety of artichoke. Italy is the leading artichoke-producing country, followed by Spain and France. The autumn harvest represents about 80 per cent of the total. The most common Italian varieties of artichoke are:

- the Sicilian variety from Catania with a cylindrical shape, which grows in autumn and winter;
- the thorny variety from Sardinia, which grows from October to May;
- the thorny variety from Liguria, which grows from October to April;
- the purple variety from San Ferdinando di Puglia, which grows from October to January;
- the Tuscany violet artichoke, which is fairly small and grows in spring;
- the large romanesco artichoke, also called *mammola*, which grows in spring. It is ideal for making artichokes *alla giudea* (Jewish-style), a typical Roman dish, or an *antipasti* of artichoke hearts.

HOW TO EAT THEM

If you are in Venice in the springtime, take the opportunity to taste the different local varieties and the multiple ways of preparing them: raw, pan-fried, deep-fried, braised! For your home-made artichoke dishes, if you can't find Venetian artichokes, use the small purple artichokes from Provence, which are just as good.

HOW TO PREPARE THEM

To trim (or 'turn') an artichoke, cut off the top 2 cm (¾ inch), remove the toughest (green) leaves using a knife or by hand, dropping the artichokes as you go into a bowl filled with lemon water (use the juice of 1 lemon) so they don't discolour, then cut them as instructed in the recipe. You can also eat the artichoke stems: peel and dice them and cook them with the artichokes.

INSALATA DI CARCIOFI CRUDI

RAW ARTICHOKE SALAD

Choose extra-fresh artichokes for this salad, which always surprises with its originality, freshness and taste of spring!

SERVES 6 PREPARATION TIME: 15 MINUTES

Trim **12 castraure artichokes** (or 6 purple artichokes) as explained on page 200 and slice them thinly just before dressing them with **120 ml (4 fl oz) olive oil** beaten with **the juice of 1 lemon, salt, pepper and 1 tablespoon chopped parsley**. Serve with shavings of **parmesan cheese**.

CARCIOFI FRITTI

DEEP-FRIED ARTICHOKES

Exquisite and unforgettable as an aperitif snack, these little deep-fried artichokes are almost exclusively served in good restaurants. They're hard to find on the counter of a bàcari! Here's a recipe to make at home.

SERVES 6 PREPARATION TIME: 30 MINUTES
COOKING TIME: 10 MINUTES

Trim **12 small purple artichokes** as explained on page 200, then cut them into quarters. In a deep-fryer or large heavy-based saucepan, heat **1 litre (35 fl oz/4 cups) of oil** to 180°C (350°F), or until a cube of bread dropped into the oil turns golden brown in 15 seconds. In a mixing bowl, combine **100 g (3½ oz/⅔ cup) of plain (all-purpose) flour** with **200 ml (7 fl oz) of iced soda water** to make a batter the consistency of a crepe batter. Dip the artichoke quarters in the batter then deep-fry them in the hot oil in small batches. Fry until golden and crisp. Drain them on paper towels and serve with a pinch of salt.

CARCIOFI SALTATI

SAUTÉED ARTICHOKES

For enjoying with pasta, risotto or as a side dish.

SERVES 6 PREPARATION TIME: 15 MINUTES
COOKING TIME: 10 MINUTES

Trim **12 small artichokes** as explained on page 200, then cut them into quarters. Heat **3 tablespoons of oil** in a frying pan with **1 garlic clove** (remove after cooking). Pan-fry the artichokes on high heat, stirring. After 2 minutes, add **2½ tablespoons of stock** or water, season with salt and finish cooking on medium heat, for about 5 minutes. Sprinkle with **chopped parsley**. The artichokes should stay crisp!

FONDI DI CARCIOFI

BRAISED ARTICHOKE HEARTS

Artichoke hearts are sold ready to cook! You notice them straight away at the vegetable stalls, floating in basins of lemon water. In Venice they are eaten almost all year round. They are often found on the counters of the bàcari at aperitif time.

SERVES 6 PREPARATION TIME: 10 MINUTES
COOKING TIME: 20 MINUTES

Heat **3 tablespoons olive oil** in a saucepan on medium heat with **1 garlic clove**, and **a handful of parsley stalks**, then add **6 artichoke hearts**. After 1 minute, add **2 cm (¾ inch) of water** (or replace 2½ tablespoons of the water with white wine), season with **salt**, cover and cook on low heat until they are tender (about 20 minutes). Add some **chopped parsley leaves**, remove the lid and allow the rest of the water to evaporate.

I PISELLI

PEAS

Known since Greek and Roman times, peas are referred to in several cookbooks dating from the fourteenth century in Italy. Louis XVI and his court were as wild about them as asparagus and artichokes. The French fashion for these vegetables was brought back from Italy.

Peas, *bisi* in Venetian, hold an important place in the gastronomy of Veneto. They are considered the 'prince of the kitchen garden'. In Scorzè, near Venice, a 'Sagra del biso' (pea festival) has been held for the last 30 years between late May and early June.

Choose small peas, which cook better than larger ones. When they are very fresh, they can be eaten raw. For 500 g (1 lb 2 oz) shelled weight of peas, allow 1 kg (2 lb 4 oz) unshelled weight. Don't throw out the pods! Clean them, cook them in a little water, then blend them into a purée to add to risotto!

Pictured opposite is the vegetable garden of the Tenuta Venissa estate in Mazzorbo.

BRAISED PEAS

For 4-6 people, blanch **500 g (1 lb 2 oz) shelled peas** for 1 minute. Heat **2 tablespoons of olive oil** in a saucepan on medium heat and sauté **1 finely chopped onion**, and **70 g (2½ oz) chopped pancetta or prosciutto** for 4 minutes, then stir in the peas. After 2 minutes, add **2½ tablespoons stock** or water, **1 tablespoon chopped parsley** and cook on low heat (approximately 10 minutes depending on their size). Season with salt. Serve with pasta or as a side dish.

RADICCHIO DI TREVISO TARDIVO

RADICCHIO TARDIVO

Radicchio tardivo belongs to the chicory family. Gastronomes love the crunch of this raw salad leaf as well as its flavour, which has a light and pleasant bitterness. Raw or cooked, grilled or sautéed, it is exquisite! It has long, fleshy, crunchy leaves, red at the tips and white near the heart. Radicchio tardivo is a highly refined product. It is the result of the expertise of a specific region around Treviso: sown in August, harvested in November, radicchio tardivo requires a 'forcing' stage that reduces its bitterness and makes it more tender. The outer leaves are removed and only the heart of the lettuce is kept.

HOW TO ENJOY THEM

Clean the root, removing all but 1 cm (½ inch), cut the radicchio into 4–6 pieces lengthways, then wash. For 6 people, allow 1 kg (2 lb 4 oz) of radicchio. Radicchio is eaten raw in salads, sautéed to flavour risotto, pasta, ravioli and lasagne, or grilled as a side dish.

HOW TO COOK THEM

Sauté **1–2 French shallots** in a frying pan in a little **olive oil** for 3 minutes. Add the **radicchio**, cut into 2–3 cm (¾–1 inch) pieces, cook on medium heat for 2 minutes, then add **a few tablespoons of red wine** and cook for another 5 minutes. Season with **salt and pepper**.

To cook in the oven, Preheat the oven to 200ºC (400ºF/Gas 6) or heat the oven grill, cut the radicchio into 2–4 pieces, brush with olive oil and season with salt and pepper. Arrange on a baking tray, and cook for about 10 minutes. Turn halfway through cooking.

INSALATA DI RADICCHIO E FAGIOLI

RADICCHIO TARDIVO & BEAN SALAD

*A happy marriage, the crunch of the radicchio works wonderfully with
Lamon or borlotti beans, which can also be served as a cold or warm purée!
Just add a drizzle of a delicate olive oil (from Lake Garda), freshly ground
black pepper, a dash of good red wine vinegar and ... happiness is yours!*

SERVES 6 PREPARATION TIME: 15 MINUTES COOKING TIME: 2 HOURS
SOAKING TIME: 8 HOURS

300 g (10½ oz) dried Lamon or borlotti beans, or fresh beans in their pods
1 onion
1 bay leaf
1 pinch of bicarbonate of soda (baking soda), or kombu seaweed
600 g (1 lb 5 oz) radicchio tardivo (see page 208), or other red
   radicchio, inside leaves only, separated
3 tablespoons mild olive oil
1 teaspoon red wine vinegar, or good balsamic vinegar

The night before, soak the dried beans in water. In the morning, discard
the leftover water and pour the beans into a saucepan. Cover them with
fresh cold water, add the whole peeled onion, bay leaf and bicarbonate
of soda, or better still some kombu seaweed, to make them more
digestible. Cook them on a very gentle simmer for about 2 hours: they
should be tender. Season with salt. Wash the radicchio, combine with
the beans. Dress with olive oil and vinegar, and salt and pepper.

VARIATIONS

You can put some of the beans through a food mill to remove their skins, thin out
the resulting purée with a little of the cooking water and spoon it into the bottom
of the serving dish (it will be better warm).

Dress the beans with *peverada* sauce (see page 174).

L'INSALATA

SALAD GREENS

In Venice, the market stalls offer a wide selection of *insalatine*—baby lettuce leaves, rocket, *valeriana* (mâche lettuce), and so on. Choose a mixture of different kinds for a variety of flavours and textures. During the cold season, you must try the *rosa di Castelfranco* and the radicchio tardivo (see page 208). In Italy, vinaigrette is not made in advance. The salad is dressed at the last moment with salt, vinegar or lemon, and olive oil (extra virgin, first cold pressed).

LE ERBE SELVATICHE

WILD GREENS

Wild greens are widely used in Italian cooking. Wash them, cook them on low heat with a little olive oil, a clove of garlic, salt and a little water. Cook them to add to a frittata, risotto, ravioli or lasagne. Dandelion and poppy shoots can be scalded before sautéeing for a few minutes in olive oil and garlic.

The main varieties found in Venice are *carletti* or *sciopeti* (bladder campion), *bruscandoli* (wild hop shoots), *tarassaco* (dandelion) and *rosoline* (poppy shoots).

In the spring, we feast on *agretti*, also called *barba di frate* (monk's beard). They are thin green stalks that look like a fleshier version of chives. Crisp and tart, *agretti* have a flavour similar to English spinach. Simmer or steam them until *al dente* for 8 minutes, and enjoy them cold as a starter or side dish, dressed with olive oil, lemon, salt and pepper.

ERBE COTTE

COOKED GREENS

This mixture of cooked greens is a typical side dish for meat or fish. It can contain *spinaci* (English spinach), *bietole* (silverbeet/Swiss chard), *catalogna o cicoria* (chicory), local greens such as *rosoline* (poppy shoots) and *tarassaco* (dandelion). They are scalded, then sautéed in olive oil, garlic, salt and pepper, or simply dressed with olive oil and lemon. This mixture is also ideal for stuffing ravioli!

VERZE

SAVOY CABBAGE

A tasty winter side dish to serve with 'rich'-tasting meat dishes, such as guinea fowl (see page 174). The traditional recipe calls for the **cabbage** to be baked very slowly (2 hours), covered, with **185 ml (6 fl oz/¾ cup) of stock**. The volume of the cabbage is reduced by a quarter and its colour turns coppery, hence the name *verze sofegae*, 'smothered cabbage' (by the long cooking)! Reduce the juices at the end of the cooking.

Remove the toughest outer leaves of the **cabbage**, cut the head into quarters, then into pieces. Sauté **1 chopped onion, 1 garlic clove** (which will be removed after cooking), some **rosemary** and **a slice of chopped bacon** or pancetta for 5 minutes in **olive oil** in a heavy-based saucepan on medium heat. Add the cabbage, season with **salt and pepper** and cook until just tender. Set the cabbage aside and reduce the cooking liquid on medium heat.

ZUCCA ARROSTA

ROAST PUMPKIN

Or *suca rosta* as they say in Venetian! The pumpkins from Chioggia, next to Venice, are famous for their tasty flesh. You can recognise them by their knobbly skin. They are perfect for risotto, ravioli, or just cut into slices and baked at 200°C (400°F/Gas 6) with rosemary, salt and a little olive oil until tender (about 40 minutes). The seeds can be toasted in the oven after being cleaned and seasoned with salt.

FLAN DI ZUCCA
PUMPKIN FLAN

It's worth the trip! Go and taste the flan di zucca at La Zucca restaurant, you will not be disappointed. A very tasty variety of pumpkin is grown in Veneto, I always brings one home with me in my suitcase. Alternatively, use a hokkaido or butternut pumpkin.

SERVES 6 PREPARATION TIME: 30 MINUTES COOKING TIME: 1½ HOURS
RESTING TIME: 15 MINUTES

80 g (2¾ oz) butter
10 sage leaves, chopped
1 kg (2 lb 4 oz) pumpkin (winter squash), peeled and cut into small cubes
250 g (9 oz) mascarpone cheese
100 g (3½ oz) potato starch (Maizena brand)
1 teaspoon freshly grated nutmeg
1 teaspoon ground cinnamon
4 eggs
Home-made breadcrumbs
80 g (2¾ oz) smoked ricotta cheese, or pecorino or parmesan cheese
1 handful of dry-roasted pepitas (pumpkin seeds)

Preheat the oven to 180°C (350°F/Gas 4). Melt 50 g (1¾ oz) of the butter with the chopped sage leaves and let them infuse off the heat. Cook the pumpkin in a large covered saucepan on low heat with 20 g (¾ oz) of the butter, salt and pepper, until very tender. Purée the pumpkin then cool. Add the mascarpone, potato starch and spices, incorporate the eggs, one at a time, and mix well. Butter individual flan moulds or ramekins, sprinkle them with breadcrumbs and fill them with the flan mixture. Place the dishes in a baking tin and pour in enough hot water to come halfway up the sides. Bake for 1 hour and 10 minutes. Let stand for 15 minutes before turning out onto plates, drizzle with the sage-flavoured melted butter (reheat if necessary), and coarsely grate over the smoked ricotta. Sprinkle with the roasted pepitas.

ERBETTE RAVE

CHIOGGIA BEETROOT

*Erbette rave are round beetroot that are a beautiful light
red colour, of the Chioggia variety selected by Venetian
horticulturists. They are eaten cooked and in salads. I prefer
to cook them al dente, so they are still firm to the bite.*

SERVES 6 PREPARATION TIME: 15 MINUTES COOKING TIME: 30 MINUTES

6 Chioggia beetroot (beets)
Olive oil
Good-quality aged wine vinegar
A little chopped flat-leaf (Italian) parsley
Salt and pepper

Wash the beetroot well and cook them in their skins in salted water, starting
them off in cold water (allow 20–30 minutes). They can also be steamed.
Check if they are cooked by piercing them with a knife. When they are
tender, drain and cool. Peel the beetroot and cut into thin slices, dress with
olive oil, a little good vinegar, chopped parsley and salt and pepper.

FINOCCHI AL LATTE

FENNEL IN MILK

*Fennel is very popular in Veneto. It is enjoyed raw as
a salad, baked as a gratin with parmesan cheese, or
braised in milk, which is surprising and delicious!*

SERVES 6 PREPARATION TIME: 20 MINUTES COOKING TIME: 25 MINUTES

6 long fennel bulbs (see note below), tough outer layer removed and trimmed
20 g (¾ oz) butter
3 tablespoons olive oil
300 ml (10½ fl oz) milk

Place the fennel bulbs in a saucepan of cold water. Bring to the boil,
add salt and cook for 3 minutes. Cool the fennel and cut each one into
6 wedges. Heat the butter and oil on medium heat in a saucepan and
sauté the fennel on all sides. Cover with the milk, season with salt and
pepper, and cook for about 15 minutes until the juices become thick.

VARIATION: FENNEL GRATIN

Preheat the oven to 180°C (350°F/Gas 4). Simmer or steam the fennel, cut
into 6 wedges and dress with olive oil. Arrange the wedges in an oiled dish,
cover with parmesan cheese and dots of butter and bake until golden brown.

NOTE

Learn to tell the difference between the male fennel bulb, which is round and better
raw, and the long female bulb, which is better cooked! During the Renaissance,
the nobility served fennel raw at the end of the meal for its digestive properties.

CARDI GRATINATI

CARDOON GRATIN

Towards the end of autumn, Venetians feast on cardoons. Their sweet and delicate flavour is similar to artichokes. Choose the very pale and fleshy bunches, the green ones are too tough and bitter! Peel them to remove the fibres. It's best to wear gloves so you don't stain your hands. Once boiled, they are braised or baked as a gratin.

SERVES 6 PREPARATION TIME: 40 MINUTES
COOKING TIME: 1¼ TO 1¾ HOURS

1.5 kg (3 lb 5 oz) cardoons
Juice of 2 lemons
1 heaped tablespoon plain (all-purpose) flour
Butter, for greasing dish
70 g (2½ oz) parmesan cheese, grated

THE BÉCHAMEL SAUCE
40 g (1½ oz) butter
40 g (1½ oz) plain (all-purpose) flour
500 ml (17 fl oz/2 cups) milk
Freshly grated nutmeg

To make the béchamel sauce: Melt the butter in a saucepan over low heat and sprinkle in the flour, stirring to combine. When the mixture starts to colour, add the milk, stirring constantly to prevent lumps, and cook for 10 minutes on low heat. Season with salt and nutmeg. Cover the surface with plastic wrap and allow to cool.

Remove any damaged cardoon stalks and the toughest outside stalks, separate the stalks from the heart one by one. Remove the fibres and the serrated part using a vegetable peeler or knife. Drop them into lemon water (add the juice of half a lemon), or rub them with lemon to prevent them from discolouring. Cut into pieces that will fit into the baking dish.

Preheat the oven to 200°C (400°F/Gas 6). Drop the cardoon pieces into a large saucepan of cold water, add the flour and the remaining lemon juice and bring to the boil, add salt and cook until they are tender (45 minutes or more). Drain the cardoons, arrange them in a buttered ovenproof dish, cover with the béchamel sauce and parmesan, then bake them in the oven for 20 minutes, or until browned.

VARIATIONS

Once cooked, dress the cardoons with 50 g (1¾ oz) melted butter, sprinkle with grated nutmeg and 50 g (1¾ oz) grated parmesan cheese. Bake in the oven for about 15 minutes at 190°C (375°F/Gas 5).

Sauté the cooked cardoons, cut into 5 cm (2 inch) sections, with a chopped onion in 30 g (1 oz) butter and 2 tablespoons olive oil for 10 minutes on medium heat. Pour over 185 ml (6 fl oz/¾ cup) of milk and reduce. At the end of the cooking time, add 1 teaspoon of chopped parsley and 20 g (¾ oz) grated parmesan cheese.

LE ZUCCHINE

ZUCCHINI

In Veneto and in Italy in general, zucchini are eaten when very small (about 10 cm/4 inches long and 2 cm/¾ inch across), so they are very sweet and almost seedless. They are enjoyed raw and grated in salads, or diced and pan-fried for 3 minutes in olive oil flavoured with garlic. They should still be crisp!

FIORI DI ZUCCHINA FARCITI

STUFFED ZUCCHINI FLOWERS

When spring comes, it's a pleasure to eat zucchini flowers stuffed, fried or baked. They are delicious, especially when they come from the gardens of Sant'Erasmo.

SERVES 6 PREPARATION TIME: 20 MINUTES COOKING TIME: 20 MINUTES

18 zucchini (courgette) flowers
8 small zucchini (courgettes), or 3 medium, cleaned and finely diced
80 ml (2½ fl oz/⅓ cup) olive oil
2 marjoram sprigs, or thyme
250 g (9 oz) ricotta cheese
100 g (3½ oz) parmesan cheese, grated
Freshly grated nutmeg
1 tablespoon fine, home-made breadcrumbs

Preheat the oven to 170°C (325°F/Gas 3). Place the zucchini flowers on paper towels, don't wash them (it will damage them!), gently open them on one side using your fingers and remove the pistil. Sauté the zucchini in a frying pan with 2 tablespoons of the oil and a marjoram sprig on medium heat for 3 minutes. Season with salt and pepper. Combine the zucchini with the ricotta and parmesan, flavour with grated nutmeg and season with salt and pepper. Using 2 small spoons, fill the zucchini flowers with the mixture and close up the flower by twisting it. Place the stuffed flowers on a baking tray lined with baking paper, sprinkle with breadcrumbs and pour over the remaining olive oil. Bake for 10-12 minutes.

DEEP-FRIED VERSION

For the batter, combine 100 g (3½ oz/⅔ cup) sifted plain (all-purpose) flour and about 185 ml (6 fl oz/¾ cup) iced soda water to make a mixture the consistency of crepe batter. In a deep-fryer or large heavy-based saucepan, heat 1 litre (35 fl oz/4 cups) of frying oil to 180°C (350°F), or until a cube of bread dropped into the oil turns golden brown in 15 seconds. Dip the flowers (stuffed or plain) in the batter, drain to remove excess batter and deep-fry them in the oil. Drain them on paper towels. Serve hot.

MELANZANE AL FUNGHETTO

SAUTÉED EGGPLANT

The appearance of eggplant in the vegetable gardens of the Venetian lagoon dates back to the fifteenth and sixteenth centuries. The Jewish community in the Venice Ghetto ate it a great deal, like most other vegetables, because of the dietary restrictions of their religion. Before this time, eggplants were considered to be evil plants. Their Italian name, melanzane, comes from the Latin malum insanum.

SERVES 6 PREPARATION TIME: 10 MINUTES COOKING TIME: 30 MINUTES

1.25 kg (2 lb 12 oz) long eggplants (aubergines)
1 garlic clove
Olive oil
½ a bunch of flat-leaf (Italian) parsley, chopped

Wash and dry the eggplants, cut them into quarters lengthways and then into cubes. Sauté the garlic on low heat in some oil in a saucepan, add the cubes of eggplant and cook gently, uncovered, for about 30 minutes, stirring often and gently. Remove the garlic, sprinkle with parsley and serve hot as a side to a meat dish.

NOTE

The name of the recipe, *funghetto*, means 'little mushroom'. When cooked, the eggplant does look like mushrooms!

PEPERONATA

STEWED CAPSICUM

When it's summer and the capsicums are in season (pevaroni in Venetian), it's time to make peperonata. The capsicums are stewed with onion, tomato sauce, basil and sometimes pieces of eggplant. The result is a delicious dish to serve with meat or pasta, or it can simply be enjoyed on good bread, as at the restaurant La Zucca!

SERVES 6 PREPARATION TIME: 15 MINUTES COOKING TIME: 45 MINUTES

2 red capsicums (peppers)
2 yellow capsicums (peppers)
3 tablespoons olive oil, plus extra for drizzling
3 red onions, finely diced
1 small eggplant (aubergine), diced
1 bunch of basil
4 tomatoes, peeled, seeded and diced (see note page 96),
    or 1 x 400 g (14 oz) tin peeled tomatoes

Cut the capsicums into chunks, removing the white membranes and seeds. In a large heavy-based saucepan, heat the olive oil and add, in this order, the onions, capsicums, eggplant, a few basil leaves and finally the tomato. Cook on low heat. As soon as the mixture comes to the boil, season with salt and stir. Continue cooking on low heat, stirring from time to time (allow about 40 minutes cooking time). At the end of the cooking time, add the remaining basil, torn, and a drizzle of olive oil.

VARIATION 'IN SALSA'

Cut 6 capsicums into 1 cm (½ inch) strips and simmer them for 5 minutes in water with a little vinegar added. Set aside. Cut 3 celery stalks and 2 carrots into pieces the same size and simmer them for 5 minutes in the capsicum cooking liquid. Drain and purée the celery and carrots, adding half a clove of crushed garlic, 2 sardines or desalted anchovy fillets, cut into small pieces, and a few spoonfuls of olive oil. Check the salt level. Dress the capsicum with this sauce.

ASPARAGI BIANCHI E VERDI

WHITE AND GREEN ASPARAGUS

Veneto is asparagus country! It has some very famous varieties such as the white asparagus from Bassano del Grappa, Padova, Cimadolmo and Badoere (Treviso), whose green asparagus also has a PGI (Protected Geographical Indication) label! Asparagus are cooked in a tall saucepan fitted with a basket (all gastronomes have one!). Steamed asparagus are served with eggs basote, still yellow and soft inside and mashed with a fork. The dish is dressed with a delicate olive oil (from Lake Garda) and a dash of good wine vinegar.

UOVA E ASPARAGI

EGGS & ASPARAGUS

SERVES 6 PREPARATION TIME: 15 MINUTES COOKING TIME: 25 MINUTES

1.5 kg (3 lb 5 oz) white asparagus
6 organic eggs
Mild olive oil
Good wine vinegar

Without touching the tip, peel the asparagus by scraping the spears with a knife from the top to the bottom to remove the fibres. Tie the asparagus in a bundle, place in a large saucepan of cold water, bring to the boil, add salt, cover and simmer gently for 10-15 minutes, depending on their size, or until just tender. Remove the asparagus from the cooking water (which can be kept for cooking the eggs), place them on a dish and keep warm under a clean cloth. Add the eggs to the simmering water and remove them after 7 minutes: the yolk needs to stay soft. Stop the cooking process by running the eggs under cold water and carefully peel them. Mash them with a fork, season with a little salt, pepper, olive oil and a dash of vinegar. Mix together and serve on the asparagus tips.

VARIATIONS

Dress boiled white and green asparagus with melted butter, place them in a baking dish, sprinkle with parmesan cheese mixed with a few breadcrumbs and brown under the oven grill.

Cut the asparagus in half lengthways, and then into thin slices (lengthways again) about 3 mm (⅛ inch) thick. Sauté them for 1 minute in olive oil. Season with salt and pepper.

ON THE DOLCI MENU

DOLCI

VENETIAN DESSERTS, CAKES AND BISCUITS

TIRAMISÙ

This dessert has travelled around the world! Its history is fairly recent, however. It was the pastry chef at the Beccherie restaurant in Treviso, Veneto, who, in the late 1960s, developed the recipe for tiramisù as it is eaten today. Its name means 'pick me up'. Tiramisù is a pick-me-up in many ways—it lifts your spirits; high in calories, it pushes up the scales; and its coffee recharges our batteries.

SERVES 8-10 PREPARATION TIME: 30 MINUTES
RESTING TIME: AT LEAST 4 HOURS

150 g (5½ oz/⅔ cup) caster (superfine) sugar
5 organic eggs, whites and yolks separated
500 g (1 lb 2 oz) mascarpone cheese
About 400 g (14 oz) savoiardi (ladyfinger) biscuits*
400 ml (14 fl oz) strong espresso coffee, at room temperature
2 tablespoons cocoa powder

Whisk 120 g (4¼ oz) of the sugar with the egg yolks using an electric beater until light and foamy. Add the mascarpone and beat to combine. In a separate bowl, whisk the egg whites to stiff peaks with a pinch of salt. After 1 minute, add the remaining sugar. Gently incorporate the egg whites into the mascarpone mix by hand with a whisk, folding from top to bottom. Dip the biscuits in the coffee for a few seconds on both sides (make sure they are not too soggy or too dry!) and place half in a layer in the bottom of a dish or dessert cups. Top with a layer of mascarpone cream and repeat the process, finishing with a layer of mascarpone cream. Refrigerate for at least 4 hours or preferably overnight. Serve lightly dusted with cocoa powder.

VARIATION

Add one or two shots of liqueur to the coffee (dry Marsala, amaretto, rum or whisky).

NOTE

A good tiramisù is made with fresh, good-quality ingredients. Excellent strong espresso coffee, extra fresh organic eggs, delicious biscuits (Italian savoiardi) and above all a good mascarpone! In northern Italy, fresh mascarpone is used (except in summer), but it doesn't travel well. Outside of Italy, one has to make do with the commercial product. To give it more flavour, I add dry Marsala.

* Also known as sponge finger biscuits in Australia.

PINZA

POLENTA CAKE WITH DRIED FRUIT

A dish with peasant roots, this is a rustic and very nourishing Epiphany dessert based on polenta and dried fruit. When I was little, country people would cook this cake in the embers of fires lit in the fields on the night of 5 January, the night they burned the befana (the effigy of the previous year) to bring good luck. This is a recipe inspired by my Auntie Tali's version …

MAKES 1 TRAY PREPARATION TIME: 30 MINUTES
COOKING TIME: ABOUT 1 HOUR

300 g (10½ oz) raisins
100 ml (3½ fl oz) grappa, or eau-de-vie
1 litre (35 fl oz/4 cups) milk
300 g (10½ oz) polenta (cornmeal)
300 g (10½ oz) caster (superfine) sugar
200 g (7 oz) dried figs, chopped
100 g (3½ oz/⅔ cup) pine nuts
50 g (1¾ oz) fennel seeds
100 g (3½ oz) butter, softened
200 ml (7 fl oz) olive oil, plus extra to oil the tray
Grated zest and juice of 1 organic orange
Grated zest of 1 organic lemon
1.3 kg (3 lb/8⅔ cups) organic strong flour
14 g (½ oz) organic baking powder
1 teaspoon bicarbonate of soda (baking soda)
100 g (3½ oz) home-made breadcrumbs

Preheat the oven to 180°C (350°F/Gas 4). Combine the raisins and grappa in a bowl and set aside for 20 minutes, then drain. Bring the milk to the boil and add 2 pinches of salt. Pour in the polenta in a stream and cook it for 5 minutes. Off the heat, add the sugar, the drained raisins, figs, pine nuts, fennel seeds, butter, oil, orange and lemon zests and orange juice. Allow the mixture to cool. Combine the flour, baking powder and bicarbonate of soda then gradually add to the polenta mixture until it is fairly firm. Mix together well with your hands or use an electric mixer. Oil a baking tray and sprinkle with the breadcrumbs. Spread out the dough to 4 cm (1½ inches) thick. Bake for about 1 hour: the cake should be dense. Cool and cut into small slices.

ZONCHIADA
RICOTTA TARTS

A classic sweet whose origins date back to the Middle Ages. A zonchiada is a delicious ricotta tart which takes its name from giuncata, a ricotta-style cheese.

SERVES 6-8 (OR 1 DOZEN TARTS)
PREPARATION TIME: 40 MINUTES RESTING TIME: 1 HOUR (OR OVERNIGHT)
COOKING TIME: 40 MINUTES TO 1 HOUR

50 g (1¾ oz) raisins
185 ml (6 fl oz/¾ cup) dry Marsala, or rum
500 g (1 lb 2 oz) ricotta cheese
2 organic eggs
100 g (3½ oz) organic raw (demerara) sugar
40 g (1½ oz) butter, melted, plus extra for greasing tins
1 teaspoon ground cinnamon
Grated zest of 1 organic lemon
50 g (1¾ oz) candied citron, diced

THE SHORTCRUST PASTRY
250 g (9 oz/1⅔ cups) organic plain (all-purpose) flour
120 g (4¼ oz) butter, softened and cut into small pieces
2 organic egg yolks
80 g (2¾ oz) organic raw (demerara) sugar
2 pinches of ground cinnamon
2-3 tablespoons dry Marsala or water

To make the pastry: Sift the flour onto your work surface and, using your fingertips, rub in the butter to make a coarse crumbly mixture. Make a well in the mixture and add the egg yolks, then the sugar, a pinch of salt, the cinnamon and Marsala or water. Combine all the ingredients using your fingertips and bring the dough together without working it too much. Form a ball and flatten it to 3 cm (1¼ inches), wrap in plastic wrap and let it rest in the refrigerator for at least 1 hour (you can also make it the day before). Work the pastry again for 30 seconds when you take it out to soften it and then roll it out on a floured work surface. Line a tray of buttered and floured tartlet moulds (or a 22-24 cm/8½-9½ inch spring-form cake tin) with the pastry, prick the bases with a fork and set aside for 15 minutes in the refrigerator.

Preheat the oven to 160°C (315°F/Gas 2-3). Place the raisins and Marsala in a bowl and set aside for 20 minutes. Mix the ricotta with a spatula until smooth. Incorporate the eggs, sugar, melted butter, cinnamon, lemon zest, citron, raisins and Marsala. Pour this mixture into the pastry case(s). Using your fingers, push down the edges of the pastry to the level of the filling. Cook in a hot oven for about 40 minutes for individual tartlets or 1 hour for a large tin.

ZALETTI
VENETIAN POLENTA BISCUITS

The name of this typically Venetian biscuit comes from the inclusion of yellow polenta (gialla in Italian) as an ingredient, which would have given gialletti and then zaletti. In the second half of the eighteenth century they were sold by street vendors during Carnevale and Carlo Goldoni refers to them in one of his comedies. These days they are delightfully available throughout the year in bakeries and pasticcerias.

MAKES ABOUT 20 BISCUITS PREPARATION TIME: 20 MINUTES
RESTING TIME: 1¼ HOURS COOKING TIME: 15 TO 20 MINUTES

50 g (1¾ oz) raisins
2½ tablespoons grappa, or eau-de-vie
125 g (4½ oz) fine polenta (cornmeal)
125 g (4½ oz) plain (all-purpose) flour
½ teaspoon organic baking powder
80 g (2¾ oz) cold butter, cut into small pieces
100 g (3½ oz) caster (superfine) sugar
1 whole egg + 1 yolk
Zest of 1 organic lemon
1 pinch of vanilla powder or ¼ teaspoon natural vanilla extract

Soak the raisins in the grappa with a little added water. Combine the polenta, flour, baking powder and a pinch of salt. In a mixing bowl, combine the butter with the sugar until you have a coarse crumbly mixture, add the whole egg and egg yolk and mix them together. Add the flour and polenta mixture to the bowl with the grated lemon zest and vanilla and knead together without overworking the dough. Add the drained raisins and knead to mix through. Let the dough rest for at least 1 hour in the refrigerator. Preheat the oven to 170°C (325°F/Gas 3) fan-forced. Roll the dough into 3-5 cm (1¼-2 inch) thick sausages, cut them on the diagonal every 7 cm (2¾ inches) and shape the pieces into small oval-shaped loaves. Line a baking tray with baking paper and place the biscuits on it. Return to the refrigerator for 15 minutes. Bake for about 15 minutes until the biscuits are lightly coloured. The biscuits will be a little soft when they come out of the oven but they will harden as they cool.

NOTE

These biscuits keep in an airtight container for three weeks. They can be eaten at any time of the day!

ZALETO
£. X 100 GRAMMI
€ 2.60
PREZZO IN EURO
PER ALIMENTI

BUSSOLAI O ESSE

VENETIAN BISCUITS

The recipe for bussolai is the same as for esse, the only difference is their shape: a ring for bussolai and an 'S' shape for esse. They are typical of the island of Burano; buy them in bulk at the bakery or pasticceria. They are perfect for dunking in a sweet wine like a recioto at the end of a meal. They keep in an airtight container for three weeks.

MAKES 20-30 DEPENDING ON SHAPE PREPARATION TIME: 20 MINUTES
RESTING TIME: 1¼ HOURS COOKING TIME: 15 MINUTES

3 egg yolks
100 g (3½ oz) caster (superfine) sugar
120 g (4¼ oz) butter, softened
Seeds from ½ vanilla bean
Grated zest of 1 lemon
250 g (9 oz/1⅔ cups) flour

Whisk the egg yolks and sugar until light and fluffy. Add the softened butter, a pinch of salt, the vanilla, lemon zest and finally the sifted flour. Knead the dough without overworking it. Let it rest for 1 hour in the refrigerator. Preheat the oven to 170°C (325°F/Gas 3) fan-forced. Cut the dough into 10 cm (4 inch) sticks and make 1 cm (½ inch) sausages to form into ring or 'S' shapes. Line a baking tray with baking paper and place the biscuits on it. Return to the refrigerator for 15 minutes. Bake for about 15 minutes: keep an eye on them as they cook as they mustn't colour. They will be a little soft when they come out of the oven but they will harden as they cool.

NOTE

There is also a version of *bussolai* that is more like a grissini. These Venetian biscuits are made from a bread dough with milk replacing the water and are called *bigarani* or *ossi da morto* (dead man's bones). Their name comes from their rounded shape with a swollen end which looks like a bone!

FREGOLOTTA

ALMOND SHORTBREAD TARTS

This tart, created in 1924 at the Zizzola restaurant in Castelfranco Veneto near Treviso, has become hugely popular. It is very easy to make at home! Fregola means 'crumb' in Veneto, and a fregolotta is made from 'crumbs' of shortcrust pastry. It crumbles when you cut it with a knife, so it's simpler to break it into pieces by hand when you eat it. It is enjoyed with coffee or a glass of sweet wine. The fregolotta is similar to sbrisolona, a humble sixteenth-century dessert from the Mantua region made from polenta and flour.

SERVES 6 PREPARATION TIME: 15 MINUTES
RESTING TIME: 1 HOUR COOKING TIME: 40 MINUTES

200 g (7 oz/1⅓ cups) plain (all-purpose) flour, plus extra for dusting the tins
100 g (3½ oz) caster (superfine) sugar, plus extra for sprinkling
100 g (3½ oz) butter, softened
100 g (3½ oz) blanched almonds, roughly chopped
2 small egg yolks
Grated zest of 1 lemon
1 pinch of vanilla powder or ¼ teaspoon natural vanilla extract

Preheat the oven to 170°C (325°F/Gas 3). Combine the flour with the sugar, butter, almonds, egg yolks, lemon zest, vanilla and 2 pinches of salt: you should have a grainy mixture with pieces the size of hazelnuts. Spread the crumbly dough with your fingers into six tartlet tins (or one large round 25 cm/10 inch tin) dusted with flour, to a thickness of about 1.5 cm (⅝ inches). Let them rest for 1 hour in the refrigerator. Bake the tartlets for about 30 minutes (allow an additional 10 minutes for one large tart). Remove from the oven and let them cool a little. Sprinkle with extra sugar when they are slightly cooled. Serve at room temperature, preferably the next day!

VARIATION

For an even more crumbly dough, use hard-boiled egg yolks.

NOTE

Serve *fregolotta* with a mascarpone cream (the same as for tiramisù, see page 234) or use as a tart crust. In this case, moisten with a little fruit coulis or coffee and fill with cream (mascarpone and whipped cream, for example).

CROSTOLI

VENETIAN CROSTOLI

Crostoli (in Venetian) and fritole (or frittelle, doughnuts) are traditional Carnevale treats in Venice. In other regions of Italy, they are called cenci or chiacchere. A very thin pastry dough is cut into diamonds and deep-fried. A sixteenth-century author described them as 'doughnuts filled with wind' ...

SERVES 6 PREPARATION TIME: 30 MINUTES COOKING TIME: 15 MINUTES

100 g (3½ oz) caster (superfine) sugar
2 eggs
60 g (2¼ oz) butter, melted
185 ml (6 fl oz/¾ cup) grappa, or eau-de-vie
100 ml (3½ fl oz) milk
500 g (1 lb 2 oz/3⅓ cups) plain (all-purpose) flour
1 litre (35 fl oz/4 cups) oil, for deep-frying
Icing (confectioners') sugar, for sprinkling

Whisk the caster sugar and eggs until smooth in a mixing bowl. Add the melted butter while it's still warm then a pinch of salt, the grappa and milk. Add the flour gradually and work into a dough until it is pliable (about 10 minutes by hand, 5 minutes using an electric mixer). On a floured work surface, roll out the dough as thinly as possible. Cut out diamond shapes with a serrated pastry wheel. In a deep-fryer or large heavy-based saucepan, heat the oil to a temperature of 180°C (350°F), or until a cube of bread dropped into the oil turns golden brown in 15 seconds, and deep-fry the *crostoli* without browning them too much. Drain them on paper towels and serve sprinkled with icing sugar.

FRITOLE VENEZIANE

VENETIAN DOUGHNUTS

It's impossible to imagine Carnevale in Venice without fritole! Bartolomeo Scappi, the cook for Pope Pius V, confirmed in his 1570 book Opera dell'arte del cucinare *that fritole are indeed Venetian dolci (sweets). He flavoured them with rosewater and saffron. In the eighteenth century, fritole officially became Venice's national dessert! In one of his famous comedies, Carlo Goldoni paints a picture of i fritolere, the street vendors who made and sold the fritole in the streets of Venice.*

SERVES 6 PREPARATION TIME: 30 MINUTES
RESTING TIME: 4 HOURS COOKING TIME: 30 MINUTES

100 g (3½ oz) currants
150 ml (5 fl oz) grappa, or eau-de-vie or rum
30 g (1 oz) fresh yeast, or 15 g (½ oz/1 tablespoon) dried yeast
80 g (2¾ oz) caster (superfine) sugar
500 g (1 lb 2 oz/3⅓ cups) plain (all-purpose) flour
2 eggs, lightly whisked
Grated zest of 1 lemon
Grated zest of 1 orange
50 g (1¾ oz/⅓ cup) pine nuts
150 ml (5 fl oz) milk
2 litres (70 fl oz/8 cups) peanut oil, for deep-frying
Sugar for dusting

Soak the currants in the grappa. Dissolve the yeast in 2½ tablespoons lukewarm water with 1 teaspoon of the caster sugar. Using a spoon, mix the flour with the eggs, the remaining caster sugar, ½ teaspoon salt and the grated zests in a large bowl. Next add the yeast mixture, pine nuts, currants and grappa and milk and mix everything together until the dough becomes shiny and pliable (about 10 minutes using a spoon). If the dough is too dense, add a little milk or water. Cover the dough with a cloth and let it rise for 4 hours in a warm place. Work the dough again for a few minutes. In a deep-fryer or large heavy-based saucepan, heat the oil to 180°C (350°F), or until a cube of bread dropped into the oil turns golden brown in 15 seconds. Make balls the size of a walnut using 2 tablespoons then deep-fry them in the oil for about 8 minutes. Don't fry too many at once, as they need to have enough space to turn over. Remove with a slotted spoon when they are well browned and place them on paper towels. Serve the *fritole* hot, dusted with sugar.

NOTE

The *fritole* dough itself is not very sweet, it's the sugar sprinkled on after cooking that gives them their sweetness.

VARIATION

In Venice, you will also find *fritole* filled with cream or zabaione (see page 254)– irresistible ... to be consumed in moderation!.

POMI AL FORNO

BAKED APPLES

Apple was once one of the few fruits available in Venice. Baked apples are part of my childhood memories. Family gatherings at Carletto restaurant in Treviso were an occasion for feasting on apples baked to a beautiful caramel colour.

SERVES 6 PREPARATION TIME: 20 MINUTES COOKING TIME: 30 MINUTES

25 g (1 oz) butter, softened
50 g (1¾ oz) caster (superfine) sugar
6 reinette apples, or use golden delicious or granny smith
185 ml (6 fl oz/¾ cup) sweet wine (*recioto* or *malvasia dolce*)

Preheat the oven to 200°C (400°F/Gas 6). Combine the butter with the sugar. Wash the apples and remove their core using an apple corer. Replace 1 cm (½ inch) of core in the hole at the base of the apple and another 1 cm (½ inch) piece in the top after filling with the butter-sugar mixture. Arrange the apples in a baking dish and pour over the sweet wine. Bake for 20-30 minutes, or until soft and collapsing. Serve warm or at room temperature.

VARIATION

Add crumbled amaretti biscuits or raisins to the butter and sugar mixture and sprinkle the apples with kirsch, dry Marsala or sweet wine.

FOCACCIA VENEZIANA

VENETIAN BRIOCHE

Focaccia is a Venetian yeast cake traditionally eaten at Easter and now found all year round in Venice. It can be eaten for breakfast dipped in caffellatte (milk coffee), or for afternoon tea, plain or spread with jam. For a home-made focaccia, allow a few hours for the dough to rise, or in Venice, buy it from a good pasticceria!

MAKES 1 *FOCACCIA*, 20 CM (8 INCHES) DIAMETER
PREPARATION TIME: 30 MINUTES RESTING TIME: 1 HOUR 50 MINUTES
COOKING TIME: 40 TO 50 MINUTES

20 g (¾ oz) fresh yeast, or 10 g (¼ oz/2 teaspoons) dried yeast
200 ml (7 fl oz) milk
500 g (1 lb 2 oz/3⅓ cups) plain (all-purpose) flour
4 egg yolks
120 g (4¼ oz) butter, diced, at room temperature, plus extra for greasing tin
150 g (5½ oz) sugar
80 ml (2½ fl oz/⅓ cup) rum, kirsch and/or dry Marsala
Grated zest of 1 lemon
1 teaspoon fine salt

GLAZE
1 egg yolk
1 tablespoon milk
50 g (1¾ oz) whole blanched almonds, coarsely chopped

Combine the fresh yeast with 80 ml (2½ fl oz/⅓ cup) of the milk, warmed, in a large mixing bowl, add 150 g (5½ oz/1 cup) of the flour and knead briefly. Cover and let the dough rest for 20 minutes. Add the egg yolks, butter, sugar, the remaining flour and milk, the rum, lemon zest and salt to this mixt\ure. Knead well with your hands (or use an electric mixer with the dough hook). Cover the dough with plastic wrap and let it rise in a warm place for 1 hour. Work the dough again by hand or in the electric mixer for 1 minute. Place the dough in a greased and floured spring-form cake tin, 20 cm (8 inches) across. Cover with plastic wrap and let the dough rise again for 30 minutes. Preheat the oven to 180°C (350°F/Gas 4). Score a cross on top of the dough and brush it with the egg yolk beaten with the milk. Sprinkle with almonds and bake for 40-50 minutes: the *focaccia* is cooked when a skewer (or knife blade) inserted into the centre comes out clean.

NOTE
Traditional *focaccia* recipes involve slower rising times, in 3 phases (2 hours + 2 hours + 5 hours).

ZABAIONE GHIACCIATO

CHILLED ZABAIONE CREAM

The restorative properties of zabaione are already mentioned in a seventeenth-century recipe! It seems that the name of this dessert comes from the old Venetian trading posts on the Croatian coast, where they served zabaja, a dense and calorific 'soup' made from orgeat syrup. The zabaione was served cold, mixed with whipped cream and accompanied by baicoli, small dry Venetian biscuits.

SERVES 6 PREPARATION TIME: 30 MINUTES COOKING TIME: 10 MINUTES
RESTING TIME: AT LEAST 2 HOURS

6 extra fresh organic egg yolks, at room temperature
100 g (3½ oz) caster (superfine) sugar
150 ml (5 fl oz) dry Marsala, or a sweet wine
2 pinches of ground cinnamon
200 ml (7 fl oz) cold thin (pouring) cream for whipping

TO SERVE (ACCORDING TO PREFERENCE):
250 g (9 oz) berry coulis with 3 dry amaretti, finely crumbled; or
80 g (2¾ oz) raisins soaked in 100 ml (3½ fl oz) dry Marsala, or sweet wine for at least
    24 hours

In a stainless steel mixing bowl, whisk the egg yolks with the sugar using an electric beater until light and airy, then add the Marsala and cinnamon, continuing to whisk. Place over a saucepan of just-simmering water (it shouldn't boil) and whisk the mixture for about 10 minutes to thicken. To cool the zabaione, dip the base of the bowl in iced water and stir it gently and regularly. Whip the cream in a separate bowl. Combine the cooled zabaione with the whipped cream. Place in the freezer for at least 2 hours to set. Serve plain or with your choice of a berry coulis and amaretti on top, or raisins soaked in alcohol.

VARIATIONS

Zabaione can be served hot, warm, cold or frozen (with or without the addition of whipped cream) and eaten with dry biscuits such as *baicoli*, slices of *panettone* or *pandoro*.

SGROPPINO

LEMON SORBET, PROSECCO & GRAPPA DIGESTIF

Typical of Venice and its region, sgroppino is a refreshing mixture of lemon sorbet blended with a little prosecco and grappa (or vodka). It is served as a digestif or between a fish and meat course during long meals. It is supposed to 'dissolve' the groppo (the knot in the stomach!), hence the name sgroppino ...

For a good *sgroppino*, choose a very good artisan sorbet and good-quality alcohol. Leave the sorbet at room temperature for a few minutes to soften. Allow 2 small scoops of sorbet per person. In a mixing bowl, mash the sorbet with a fork, then stir it until smooth. Mix the sorbet into a half-and-half mix of prosecco and grappa (or vodka) until you have a smooth and fairly dense consistency. It can also be mixed in a blender. Serve in stemmed glasses.

UVETTA SOTTO GRAPPA

RAISINS IN GRAPPA

<u>MAKES</u> 6 SMALL GLASSES <u>PREPARATION TIME</u>: 5 MINUTES
<u>RESTING TIME:</u> 3 DAYS

Steep **180 g (6½ oz) raisins** in **300 ml (10½ fl oz) of grappa** in a jar for at least 3 days.

INDEX

GOURMET SHOPPING

What typical food items can you buy and bring home from Venice? Be led by your curiosity and go to the Rialto Market, a veritable temple of food. The fish market is in two old market halls overlooking the Grand Canal and next door you'll find the fruit and vegetable markets, shops selling cheeses and cured meats, butchers and the best food stores and *bàcari* in the city. Most importantly, leave a little room in your suitcases for your shopping (at bargain prices), because you'll want to buy everything! That way you'll be able to continue your gastronomic voyage back home …

FROM THE GROCERY STORE

- **Polenta** *bianca* (white polenta). White polenta is typical of Venice and Treviso. It's made from a very old variety of corn. Ask for *Bianco Perla* polenta, the variety considered to be the best quality, finer and tastier than yellow polenta. It is the essential accompaniment for the fish of the lagoon (see recipes pages 84 and 148).

- *Bigoli*. Bigoli is a thick wholemeal spaghetti that is prepared *in salsa,* with a sauce made from onion and anchovies or salted sardines (see recipe page 92).

- Some good **artisan pasta**.

- **Risotto rice** from Veneto, the local variety is called Vialone Nano.

- **Dried porcini**, **Italian saffron**, **condiments flavoured with white truffle,** all recommended ingredients for flavouring your risotto.

- A good bottle of **olive oil from Lake Garda**. It goes without saying that when I recommend an olive oil, it must be extra virgin, first cold pressed and produced from Italian olives. Thanks to the lake's microclimate, this olive oil is very delicate and refined. It is perfect for dressing fish. Ask for advice on a good **balsamic vinegar** that's been aged for a few years or the traditional balsamic vinegar that is aged for at least 12 years, a real nectar to be used sparingly, in drops.

- **Dried beans** (*fagioli secchi),* preferably the lamon or borlotti varieties (see recipes pages 138 and 210). The dried beans from Lamon, a small mountain village in Veneto, are exquisite. They have the thin skins and floury quality that is essential for soup.

CHEESES

When it comes to cheese, you have an embarrassment of choice. Ask for it to be vacuum-packed for the trip home.

- **Parmesan**. Make the most of being in Italy by buying a parmesan cheese that's been matured for 36 months. It will be perfect to enjoy as is or grated over risotto or pasta. We also produce **grana padano** in the Venice region, which can be matured for up to 24 months and is more of a table cheese.

- **Fresh asiago cheese DOP** (*Denominazione di Origine Protetta* or protected designation of origin) is enjoyed for its milky aroma. Sweet and delicate on the palate, **mature** asiago has very aromatic hay flavours. It can be a little sharp if it is very mature.

- **Monte veronese DOP** is a very aromatic cheese with floral and hay notes. It has an intense and slightly sharp flavour if it is very mature (12 months).

- **Montasio DOP** is aged between 2 and 24 months. It has a delicate and slightly herbaceous flavour. When fresh, its milky taste dominates. When it has matured, its flavour is more intense and aromatic. Montasio is a typical hard cheese that is eaten with drinks or as a snack. There are other similar cheeses from Veneto, such as **piave** and **latteria**. **Carnia** and **carnia altobut** (a mountain cheese) are cheeses from Friuli. All of these semi-hard and hard cheeses are the favourite snack of people in this region. I learned from my mother to use **latteria** instead of mozzarella on pizza. It has noticeably more flavour than a mass-produced mozzarella.

- **Ubriaco** (which means 'drunk') is a semi-hard cow's milk cheese, typical of the Treviso region. It is matured with *raboso* wines, one of the typical varieties of this province near the Piave River. The tradition of maturing the cheese in this way dates back to World War I, when the country people had the idea of hiding their cheeses in barrels of grape must so they didn't fall into the hands of the occupying forces! This richly aromatic cheese has a fruity, 'dense' flavour, with a slight sharpness. It is perfect with a good polenta.

- **Casatella** is a delicious creamy cheese, typical of Treviso, which should be eaten very fresh. It is ripened from 4–8 days. It has a very sweet milky flavour. Children adore it. It's one to enjoy on the spot because of its runny consistency.

- *Mostarda*, candied mustard fruits in essential mustard oil (Lazzaris brand), to serve with cheeses, meat (*bollito misto*, see recipe page 180) or with panettone at Christmas ...

- Luxardo brand '**marasche**' preserved cherries or cherry liqueurs to flavour your desserts.

CURED MEATS

Sopressa is a good Italian pork salami. Fresh and tender, it melts in the mouth and has a full, delicious flavour. It is only cut by knife and is perfect for filling a *piccolo panino* (a small sandwich). Ask for it to be vacuum-packed for you.

Take the opportunity while you're there to taste prosciuttos of different ages (over 14 months). The neighbouring region of Friuli produces the exquisite San Daniele prosciutto and the delicious *prosciutto di Sauris*. Emilia Romagna excels with its *culatello* and *prosciutto di Parma* ...

Ricotta

nostrana
€ 8.95 al kilo

ALCOHOL

Make certain you take home a bottle of **Venetian white wine**, a real rarity! Also remember some prosecco, an artisan **grappa** (a grape marc eau-de-vie) and aperitifs (Ramazzotti aperitivo, Select, Aperol ...) essential for your home-made spritz. Drink in moderation, excessive alcohol intake is dangerous for your health!

BISCUITS AND SWEETS

- Round **grissini** such as *bussolai* biscuits, which is where the sweet version originated (see recipe page 242). In former times they were called *pan-biscotto* (biscuit-bread) because they kept for a long time and fed the sailors. These round grissini are made from flour, olive oil, lard, malt, yeast and salt.

- Artisan crispbreads, like the extra-thin *figuli* from Visnadello (Treviso) or the irresistible **grissini** *bibanesi* made from olive oil and kamut flour, sold in supermarkets. Try the very thin artisan **Sartorelli** biscuits, with almonds or hazelnuts ... once you start eating them, it's hard to stop.

- *Baicoli*. These are delicious dry biscuits and typically Venetian. Thin and light, they're dunked in coffee or desserts. They're sold in boxes with designs on the outside that haven't changed since my childhood (a cardboard box at the supermarket, a metal box in *pasticcerias*)!

- The **mandorlato di Cologna Veneta**. This is an exquisite hard nougat. Its recipe is a hundred years old. It is made exclusively from blanched almonds, honey, sugar and egg white and cooked for 9 hours. This is a true sweet indulgence sold especially at Christmas time.

- A packet of **caffè** to dip your biscuits into.

VEGETABLES

I always bring a few kilos of vegetables home with me in my suitcase! In springtime, I buy ones grown on Sant'Erasmo (an island of the lagoon), such as **artichokes** and the little *castraure* available in April-May, sweet little **zucchini** for eating raw, grated in a salad, and sweet and tender **peas**. In the area of wild greens, I have a weakness for *carletti* and *bruscandoli* (see page 212), which are welcome additions to an omelette or risotto. I also don't forget the delicious white **asparagus** from Bassano and the *agretti* for enjoying in a salad. In winter, I bring back the fabulous *radicchio tardivo* di Treviso (see page 208).

WINES

With its favourable climate, carefully maintained traditions, suitable soil and vine craft, the Venice region has recently become Italy's largest wine producer. The traditional varieties are *rondinella*, *molinara*, *corvina veronese* and *raboso* for the reds, *garganega*, *prosecco*, *verduzzo* and *trebbiano* for the whites.

Valpolicella is one of the most famous reds. Light and fruity, it should be drunk fairly young. From the refermentation of this wine on the lees of *amarone* wines comes the *ripasso*, a much more structured and complex wine that is particularly enjoyed with meat-based *secondi piatti*, risotto with sausage and polenta. The drier, richer and more powerful *amarone*, and the amazing, sweet and opulent *recioto*, are wines for aging. One, with its strong personality, is made for autumn dishes like poultry, mature cheeses and cured meats, the other, sweet and intense, can be saved for the end of a meal or for fruit-based pastries and biscuits. The Vaona family estate, 10 km (6 miles) from Verona, maintains its vineyards in keeping with the traditional methods.

Alongside Vicenza is Gambellara, a village where the native *garganega* variety yields superb white wines. The truest and most surprising expression of the *terroir* is found in the cellar of Angiolino Maule, whose white *masieri*, *sassaia*, and *pico* wines reflect all of the natural forces. These well-structured wines go perfectly with *cicheti*, meatless *antipasti*, fish and seafood risottos and vegetable risottos.

For a more classic white that is fresh and young, try the *soave classico* from the Pieropan family in Soave (Verona), where the local *garganega* and *trebbiano* varieties make this wine a perfect all-purpose partner for the traditional dishes of the region: artichokes, pumpkin flowers, sardines, risotto and even desserts such as *fritole*.

For biscuits and dry cakes such as *fregolotta*, *zaletti*, *focaccia* and *pinza*, the sweet white *torcolato* will evoke notes of honey, dried fruit, almond and vanilla. The production area is Breganze, north of Vicenza, where a handful of wine growers ensure the continuity of this beverage in line with the traditions.

A very special mention goes to one of the rare wines from the Venice lagoon: the *orto di Venezia*. Made from a blend of very old Italian varieties (*vermentino*, *fiano* and Istrian *malvasia*), it's a minerally white wine that is especially expressive of its *terroir* and it is a perfect match with the typical dishes of the lagoon based on crustaceans, fish, artichokes and asparagus.

It is closely followed by the last-born, the *venissa* from the Bisol family cellars. After ten years of research, this winemaking family, already well known for its exceptional prosecco, gives us a unique white wine, the fruit of a local variety, the Venetian *dorona* grown in the heart of the lagoon on the Tenuta Venissa estate on Mazzorbo island (connected to Burano). Superb with bigoli and *antipasti*

with prawns, scampi and crab, this nectar, fermented for a year-and-a-half like a red wine, is produced in a very limited quantity.

The province of Treviso, north of Venice, is the home of *prosecco*, a dry sparkling white wine. It's a wine with a slightly aromatic perfume, sometimes with almond notes, it is excellent both as an aperitif and as a sparkling table wine. In addition to being one of the main ingredients of the famous Venetian aperitif, spritz, *prosecco* goes very well with soups, pasta-based *primi piatti*, fresh cheeses, duck, chicken and rabbit. The wine cellar of the Gregoletto family, between the hills of Valdobbiadene, Conegliano and Vittorio Veneto, has for centuries cultivated vines that produce a *prosecco* of exceptional quality.

More and more winemakers are taking the 'risk' of producing natural wines: no interventions on the vine. This is the origin of the organic sur lie *proseccos* produced by Casa Belfi at San Polo di Piave. It's a 'winemaker's wine' that partners well with gnocchi with duck *ragù*, pork roasted in milk and *baccalà*.

Veneto shares its wealth of grape varieties with the neighbouring region of Friuli-Venezia Giulia. Sometimes the same varieties are found there, but also other typical local varieties—*tocai friulano*, *malvasia*, *ribolla* for the whites, *refosco* and *schioppettino* for the reds.

The *verduzzo friulano* and *ribolla* whites of the I Clivi winery combine warm and complex aromas with a freshness and palatability that's characteristic of the Galea and Brazan hills. These are wines to try with local pastries, ripened and veined cheeses, and shellfish.

The organic reds of Marina Sgubin, between Gorizia and Udine, are wines of great character, traditionally light and fruity and becoming more full bodied with age. To pair with sausages and polenta, *cotechino* and game.

These regions not only produce excellent wines but also a legendary eau-de-vie: grappa. Traditionally made in northern Veneto, at Bassano del Grappa, this digestif is the result of distilling the marcs of local grapes. It is enjoyed after a good meal, by itself or to flavour a good strong coffee.

ADDRESS BOOK

CANNAREGIO PROMENADE (PAGES 48-49)

1- PASTICCERIA DAL MAS
Cannaregio 149/150
Rio Terà Lista di Spagna
Tel: +39 041 715101
closed Mondays and Tuesdays

2- PANIFICIO GIOVANNI VOLPE Jewish bakery
Calle del Ghetto Vecchio
Cannaregio 1143
Tel: +39 041 715178
closed 1 pm to 5 pm and Sundays

3- AL TIMON *cicheti*/restaurant
Fondamenta degli Ormesini
Cannaregio 2754
Tel: +39 041 5246066
closed Wednesdays
open until 1 am

4- ALLE DUE GONDOLETTE
restaurant, Fondamenta delle
Cappuccine, Cannaregio 3016
Tel: +39 041 717523
closed evenings, Saturdays
and Sundays

5- ANICE STELLATO
Fondamenta della Sensa
Cannaregio 3272
Tel: +39 041 720744
closed Mondays and Tuesdays

6- TORREFAZIONE MARCHI
café/coffee roasters
Rio Terrà San Leonardo
Cannaregio 1337
Tel: +39 041 716371
www.torrefazionemarchi.it

7- LA CANTINA wine bar
Campo San Felice, Cannaregio 3689
Tel: +39 041 5228258
closed Sundays

8- VINI DA GIGIO
Fondamenta San Felice
Cannaregio 3628a
Tel: +39 041 5285140
closed Mondays and Tuesdays
www.vinidagigio.com

9- ANTICA ADELAIDE
Calle Larga Priuli Racheta
Cannaregio 3728
Tel: +39 041 5232629

10- ALLA VEDOVA/CÀ D'ORO
Calle del Pistor, Cannaregio 3912
Tel: +39 041 5285324
closed Thursdays and
Sunday mornings

SAN POLO PROMENADE (PAGES 86-87)

1- MARCO BERGAMASCO, fishmonger
Rialto Market Pescheria
Tel: +39 335 6626115
closed Sundays and Mondays

2- PRONTO PESCE
San Polo 319
Tel: +39 041 8220298
www.prontopesce.it
closed Sundays and Mondays

3- BAR FIAMMA
San Polo 317

4- I DO MORI
Calle dei Do Mori - San Polo 429
Tel: +39 041 5225401
open from 8.30 am to 8.30 pm.
closed Sundays

5- ALL'ARCO
Calle dell'Occhialer
San Polo 436
Tel: +39 041 5205666
closed Sundays

6- CANTINA DO SPADE
Calle Do Spade
San Polo 859-860
Tel: +39 041 15210583
www.cantinadospade.com
Open every day between
3 pm and 6 pm

7- ANTICHE CARAMPANE
Rio Terà delle Carampane
- San Polo 1911
Tel: +33 041 5240165
www.antichecarampane.com
closed Sundays and Mondays

8- CASA DEL PARMIGIANO
Campo della Bella Vienna
San Polo 214
Tel: +39 041 5206525
www.aliani-casadelparmigiano.it
closed Sundays and afternoons
Monday to Thursday

9- AL MARCÀ wine bar
Campo della Bella Vienna
San Polo 213
closed Sundays

10- MASCARI grocery store
Ruga del Spezier - San Polo 381
Tel: +39 041 5229762
www.imascari.com
closed Sundays and
Wednesday afternoons

11- LAGUNA CARNI butcher
Ruga del Spezier - San Polo 315
closed afternoons and Sundays

12- CAFFÈ DEL DOGE
Calle dei cinque / San Polo 609
Tel: +39 041 5227787
open 7 am to 7 pm.
Closed Sundays

13- ALIANI delicatessen,
cheese, cured meats
ruga Rialto / ruga vecchia San
Giovanni, San Polo 654
Tel: +39 041 5224913
closed Sundays, Monday afternoons
and between 1 pm and 5 pm

14- RIZZARDINI pasticceria
Campiello dei Meloni
San Polo 1415
Tel: +39 041 5223835
closed Tuesdays

15- OSTERIA BANCOGIRO
cicheti and restaurant
Campo San Giacometto
San Polo 122
Tel: +39 041 5232061
www.osteriabancogiro.it
closed Mondays

16- ALLA MADONNA
60s restaurant
Calle della Madonna - San Polo 594
Tel: +39 041 5223824
www.ristorantealalamadonna.com

17- VECIO FRITOLIN restaurant
famous for its takeaway fried fish
Calle della Regina
Sestiere Santa Croce 2262
Tel: +39 041 5222881
www.veciofritolin.it

CASTELLO AND SAN MARCO PROMENADE (PAGES 144-145)

1- ROSA SALVA
pasticceria, ice-cream
Campo dei Santi Giovanni e Paolo
Castello 6779
Tel: +39 041 5227949
www.rosasalva.it
open daily to 8.30 pm

2- AL PONTE bar, *cicheti*
Calle larga Giacinto Gallina
Cannaregio 6378
Tel: +39 041 5286157
www.ostariaalponte.com
open from 8.30 am to 8.30 pm
closed Sundays

3- LIBRAIRIE FRANÇAISE
Calle della Barbaria delle Tole
Castello 6358
Tel: +39 041 5229659
open from 9 am to 12.30 pm
and 3.30 pm to 7.30 pm, closed
Sundays and Mondays

4- LA MASCARETA wine bar
Calle Lunga Santa Maria Formosa
Castello 5183
Tel: +39 041 5230744
open from 7 pm to 2 am
closed Wednesdays and Thursdays

5- OSTERIA ALLE TESTIERE
Calle del Mondo Novo
Castello 5801
Tel: +39 041 5227220
www.osterialletestiere.it
closed Sundays and Mondays

6- AL COVO restaurant
Campiello della Pescaria
Castello 3968
Tel: +39 041 5223812
www.ristorantealcovo.com
closed Wednesdays and Thursdays

7- CORTE SCONTA restaurant
Calle del Pestrin - Castello 3886
Tel: +39 041 5227024
closed Sundays and Mondays

8- AL TODARO ice-cream
Piazza San Marco 3
open 8 am to 8 pm

9- CAFFÈ FLORIAN
Piazza San Marco 56
Tel: +39 041 5205641
www.caffeflorian.com

10- HARRY'S BAR
Calle Vallaresso
San Marco 1323
Tel: +39 041 5285777

SANTA CROCE, DORSODURO AND GIUDECCA PROMENADE (PAGES 168-169)

1- AL PROSECCO
wine bar, wine store
Campo San Giacomo dell'Orio
Santa Croce 1503
Tel: +39 041 5240222
9 am to 8 pm, closed Sundays

2- ALASKA ice-cream
Calle larga dei Bari
Santa Croce 1159
Tel: +39 041 715211
12 noon to 10 pm, closed
Mondays in winter

3- LA ZUCCA restaurant
Ponte del Megio – Santa Croce 1762
Tel: +39 041 5241570
www.lazucca.it
closed Sundays

4- TONOLO bar-pasticceria
Calle San Pantalon – Dorsoduro 3764
Tel: +39 041 5237209
closed Sunday afternoons
and Mondays

5- CAMPO SANTA MARGHERITA
This is a large square where you will find a few trees, bars that are open until late and a small vegetable and fish market.

6- BARCA fruit and vegetables
Dorsoduro 2837, under
the Ponte dei Pugni
Tel: +39 041 5222977

7- PANTAGRUELICA
wine cellar, cured
meats, fine foods
Campo San Barnaba
Dorsoduro 2844
Tel: +39 041 5236766

8- GROM artisan ice-cream
three locations open every day from 11 am until late evening in summer:
Campo San Barnaba – Dorsoduro
San Polo, 3006 – Campo dei Frari
Cannaregio 3844 (Strada Nuova –
Cà D'Oro)

9- LA BITTA meat restaurant
Calle Lunga San Barnaba
Dorsoduro 2753a
Tel: 39 041 5230531
open in the evening, closed Sundays

10- LA FURATOLA restaurant
Calle Lunga San Barnaba
Dorsoduro 2869
Tel: +39 041 5208594
closed Sundays

11- PASTICCERIA DAL NONNO COLUSSI
Calle Lunga San Barnaba
Dorsoduro 2867a
Tel: +39 041 5231871
open from Thursday to Saturday

12- AI ARTISTI bar-restaurant
Fondamenta della Toletta
Dorsoduro 1169a
Tel: +39 041 5238944
open from 8 am to 10 pm,
closed Sundays

13- GELATI NICO ice-cream
Fondamenta Zattere ai Gesuati
Dorsoduro 922
Tel: +39 041 5225293
www.gelaterianico.com
7 am to 10 pm, closed Thursdays

14- CANTINONE GIÀ SCHIAVI
wine cellar, *cicheti* and aperitifs
Ponte San Trovaso – Dorsoduro 992
Tel: +39 041 5230034

15- LA RIVIERA restaurant
Fondamenta Zattere – San Basilio
Dorsoduro 1473
Tel: +39 041 5227621
closed Mondays

16- ALTANELLA restaurant
Calle delle Erbe – Giudecca 268
Tel: +39 041 5227780

17- FABIO GAVAGNIN
fishmonger
Giudecca 592
Tel: 041 5231222

18- IL PANIFICIO CLAUDIO CROSARA
bakery
Giudecca 657
Tel: +39 041 5206737

19- FORTUNY
art fabrics
showroom Sestiere Giudecca 805
Tel: +39 041 5287697
www.fortuny.com
closed Sundays

PROMENADE IN THE ISLANDS OF THE LAGOON, MAZZORBO AND BURANO (PAGES 192-193)

1- TENUTA VENISSA (RISTORANTE/OSTELLO)
Fondamenta Santa Caterina 3
30170 Isola di Mazzorbo
Tel: +39 041 5272281

2- AL GATTO NERO
Fondamenta Giudecca 88 – Burano
Tel: +39 041 730120

3- DA ROMANO
Piazza Galuppi 221 – Burano
Tel: +39 041 730030

OFFICIAL WEBSITE OF THE CITY OF VENICE
www.comune.venezia.it

INDEX

271

GRAZIE

To my editor and Audrey Génin, to Grégoire Kalt for his photojournalism in Venice: what good gastronomic memories!

For taking the time to be my guides in Venice: GRAZIE to Maria, Roberto, Matteo. Thank you to all those who gave me tips to good places: Betty, Valerio, Alessia, Sabina, Manuela, Michela, my brother Carlo and Martina, my cousins Alessandro and Stefano, Giuseppe Iannò, Giovanni Gregoletto.

GRAZIE for their precious support to my darling Philippe, my Venetian friend Piera Grandesso, and also to Mariolina Secco and her family, Emmanuelle Mourareau, Ariadne Elisseeff, Francesca Solarino. A big thank you to Alessandra Pierini from the RAP food store in Paris for her collaboration on the section on wine, her passion!

GRAZIE to all the *bàcari* and restaurants that helped me in making this book: Laura from Vini da Gigio, Francesco from La Cantina, Mauro Lorenzon from Mascareta, Cesare Benelli from Al Covo, Franca from Anice Stellato, Luca from Alle Testiere, the fishmonger Marco Bergamasco, Francesco from Antiche Carampane, the Pinto family at All'Arco, Matteo from Bancogiro, Stefano at Altanella, Rudy at La Zucca, Silvia at Caffè Florian, Laura at Harry's Bar, Michela Da Bona and Gian Luca Bisol at the Tenuta Venissa estate.

GRAZIE to all those who lent me supplies: Philippe Model, Alessi, Holland & Sherry for Fortuny, Bureau 110 for LSA international, Dominique Kieffer-Rubelli, and Society, and my *mamma*!

BIBLIOGRAPHY

P. Agostini and A. Zorzi, *La Table des Doges* (Tournai: Casterman, 1992).

A. Bay and S. Salvatori, *La Cucina Nazionale Italiana* (Milano: Adriano Salani Editore, 2008).

J. Clausel, *Venise exquise* (Paris: Payot, 1990).

C. Coco, *Venezia in Cucina* (Roma-Bari: Editori Laterza, 2007).

M. Gotti, *Grande Enciclopedia Illustrata della Gastronomia* (Milano: Arnoldo Mondadori Editore, 2007).

E. Grandesso, *Magna e Bevi che la Vita Xé un Lampo!* (Spinea, Venezia: Edizione Helvetia, 2007).

E. Grandesso, *Se No Xé Pan Xé Polenta* (Spinea, Venezia: Edizione Helvetia, 2005).

INSOR, *Atlante dei Prodotti Tipici: La Pasta* (Roma: Agra Editrice, 2004).

G. Maffioli, *La Cucina Veneziana* (Padova: Franco Muzio Editore, 1995).

G. Rorato, *Origini e Storia della Cucina Veneziana* (Vittorio Veneto: Dario De Bastiani Editore, 2010).

B. Scappi, *Opera*, (Venezia: Tramezzino, 1570; Bologna: Arnaldo Forni Editore, 1981).

GUIDES:

To learn more about all the restaurants and shops in Venice and the islands of the lagoon, see the guides by Michela Scibillia: *Osterie e dintorni* and *Botteghe e dintorni* or *Venice Osterie* and *Venice Botteghe* in English. There is also an iPhone edition of *Venice Osterie* – look for Tap Venice Eat in iTunes.

ALTERNATIVE ITINERARIES:

Hugo Pratt, Guido Fuga and Lele Vianello, *Venise, itinéraires avec Corto Maltese* (Casterman, 2010) or *The Secret Venice of Corto Maltese* (Rizzoli Lizard, 2005).

Thomas Jonglez and Paola Zoffoli, *Venise insolite et secrète* (Versailles: Éditions Jonglez, 2010) or *Secret Venice* (Versailles: Jonglez Publishing, 2012)

A LITTLE BOOK TO AWAKEN ALL OUR SENSES:

Tiziano Scarpa, *Venezia è un pesce* (Milano: Feltrinelli, 2000) or *Venice is a Fish* (London: Serpent's Tail, 2010).

SUPPLIERS

FORTUNY SPA
Fortuny art fabrics (page 131)
Giudecca 805, 30123 Venise
Tel: +39 041 5287697
fortuny.com - venice@fortuny.com
Paris showroom:
HOLLAND & SHERRY
17 rue de l'Échaude, 75006 Paris
Tel: 01 42 33 55 91
www.hollandandsherry.com -
info@hollandandsherry.fr

RUBELLI
'Bucolic' fabrics by Dominique Kieffer for Rubelli (pages 127, 135, 137, 161, 163, 181, 211, 215, 221)
11-13 rue de l'Abbaye, 75006 Paris
Tel: 01 56 81 20 20
www.rubelli.com - france@rubelli.com

SOCIETY, ADELE SHAW BOUTIQUE
White Society tablecloth, 'New jour' (page 132-3)
33 rue Jacob, 75006 Paris
Tel: 01 42 60 80 72
www.societylimonta.com -
adele.shaw75@orange.fr

MADERA
Wooden paddle (page 109)
Campo San Barnaba, Dorsoduro 2762
Venice, Italy / Tel: +39 041 5224181
www.maderavenezia.it

ALESSI
Plates and cutlery (pages 105, 127, 135, 137)
31 rue Boissy-D'Anglas, 75008 Paris
Tel: 01 42 66 31 00
showroom.paris@alessi.com
- www.alessi.com

LSA INTERNATIONAL
Plates, cups and ramekins (page 181)
http://www.lsa-international.com/stores

ROSENTHAL / SUOMI PLATES
Plates (page 131)
www.rosenthal.de
Leather tablecloths from
Philippe Model's collection
San Marco embroidered tablecloths and silver cutlery, from my mother's collection

First published by Hachette Livre (Marabout) in 2013.
Published by Murdoch Books in 2014, an imprint of Allen & Unwin.

Murdoch Books Australia
83 Alexander Street
Crows Nest NSW 2065
Phone: +61 (0) 2 8425 0100
Fax: +61 (0) 2 9906 2218
www.murdochbooks.com.au
info@murdochbooks.com.au

Murdoch Books UK
Erico House, 6th Floor
93–99 Upper Richmond Road
Putney, London SW15 2TG
Phone: +44 (0) 20 8785 5995
Fax: +44 (0) 20 8785 5985
www.murdochbooks.co.uk
info@murdochbooks.co.uk

For Corporate Orders & Custom Publishing contact Noel Hammond,
National Business Development Manager, Murdoch Books Australia

Publisher: Corinne Roberts
Photographer: Grégoire Kalt
Illustrations: Roxane Lagache
Translator: Melissa McMahon
Editor: Victoria Chance
Food Editor: Grace Campbell
Editorial Manager: Katie Bosher
Production: Mary Bjelobrk

Text and design © Hachette Livre (Marabout) 2013

A cataloguing-in-publication entry is available from the catalogue of the National Library of Australia at www.nla.gov.au.

A catalogue record for this book is available from the British Library.

Colour reproduction by Splitting Image, Clayton, Victoria.

Printed by 1010 Printing Group Limited, China.

IMPORTANT: Those who might be at risk from the effects of salmonella poisoning (the elderly, pregnant women, young children and those suffering from immune deficiency diseases) should consult their doctor with any concerns about eating raw eggs.

OVEN GUIDE: You may find cooking times vary depending on the oven you are using. For fan-forced ovens, as a general rule, set the oven temperature to 20°C (35°F) lower than indicated in the recipe.

MEASURES GUIDE: We have used 20 ml (4 teaspoon) tablespoon measures. If you are using a 15 ml (3 teaspoon) tablespoon add an extra teaspoon of the ingredient for each tablespoon specified.